How to Get **RICH**
Selling Banking and Brokerage Services to Women!

ADVANCE PRAISE . . .

If men are from Mars and woman are from Venus, then Rebecca & Marti are the distinguished ambassadors who can show the men of the planet how to better communicate with woman in their language. I love their book!

Robert A. Kerzner, CLU, ChFC

President & CEO
LIMRA International

We all know that women will be buying 60 percent of the financial services in the US by the year 2010. The problem we face at Sky Bank is in not understanding how to approach this opportunity. Maddox and Smye are the first to show us how to strengthen our sales culture by enhancing the sales experience for our women clients.

Marty Adams

Chairman, President and CEO
Sky Financial Group, Inc.

The Maddox Smye 12-week program and book are absolutely fantastic! We now understand and appreciate the important differences between men and women's decision-making process. It's been fun watching our sales team change their approach, apply the tools—and get results!

Patrick T. Bulger

Financial Consultant
A.G. Edwards & Sons, Inc.

This book makes just the right pitch—Rebecca and Marti have described perfectly what sales professionals need to do to be successful. With literally hundreds of great tips and tools, it's a playbook for every salesperson who comes in contact with women buyers.

Frank Murphy

Partner
Hunton and Williams LLP

CONTENTS

How to Get RICH Selling Banking and Brokerage Services to Women!

REBECCA MADDOX, M.B.A., C.P.A.

MARTI SMYE, PH.D.

Maddox Smye, LLC
Naples, Florida

maddoxsmye
wiser about women

Published by:
Maddox Smye, LLC
300 Fifth Avenue South, Suite 101
Naples, Florida 34103
www.maddoxsmye.com

Literary Agent:
Albert Zuckerman
Writers House
21 West 26th Street
New York, New York 10010

ISBN 0-9727637-3-2

PRINTED IN THE UNITED STATES OF AMERICA
10 9 8 7 6 5 4 3 2 1

ACKNOWLEDGMENTS

From Rebecca . . .

Here's a confession . . . I never wanted to be a salesperson—ever. Growing up in Ohio, daughter of Dan Maddox, a Nabisco salesman, I didn't think being in sales was a "real" profession. In my kid-view of the world, if you weren't a doctor, a lawyer, or a banker, you didn't have a real job. Almost any other career seemed infinitely more important than sales.

Time, age, and wisdom change many things, including perception.

Fortunately, the sales profession is gaining the respect it so deserves. All successful people in sales—first, and most importantly, are selling themselves. You simply can't "win" in life if you don't know the basics of selling. In sales, you make things happen. You serve other people—often saving them time and money and meeting their needs through the services and products you offer. I salute the dynamic men and women who distinguish themselves as leaders in a field that transcends other professions.

So here I am in sales, like my Dad. I've spent most of my life in corporate America selling in one form or another. Now, as an entrepreneur, I use my sales ability to persuade people to believe in me and the products and services of Maddox Smye. Thanks, Dad, for pursuing a sales vocation and demonstrating daily that serving other people is the highest calling. You've been a great role model and teacher. I only hope someday I can be as good you!

From Marti . . .

I, too, grew up in Ohio. Salineville, Ohio (population 1,397) is a little town that obviously has something good in the water—it produced me and Ben Feldman, the legendary life insurance salesman who sold more than a billion dollars' worth of life insurance during his career. He was so good at what he did that when his company, New York Life, ran a nationwide sales contest, he won by writing $15 million of new business in a month—at the age of 80.

In small towns, people understand that relationships count. The time spent on the front porch getting to know someone pays big dividends, not only for the initial sale, but for life. There are many lessons: loyalty comes from trust; trust comes from good listening; good listening comes from genuine caring.

And here's a tip for sales managers: you just might want to recruit in Salineville. I can tell you, people understand loyalty, trust, good listening and genuine caring—foundations for a salesperson. Thanks, Ben Feldman. Thanks, Salineville.

From Marti and Rebecca . . .

To all of the amazing sales professionals in our lives—men and women, personal friends, and clients—we offer a hearty "Here's to you!" You've chosen a great profession. Thanks for generously sharing your stories so we could learn from and with you. We applaud your passion for selling, your tenacity to keep on selling, and your willingness to try new approaches to make women your best, most loyal clients.

To our writer extraordinaire, Barry Schwenkmeyer, our heartfelt thanks for helping us find the right "voice." Your words, wisdom, and wit are certain to inspire our readers.

To our extraordinary staff at Maddox Smye—you are simply the best. We couldn't have done it without your remarkable ability to support us and cheer us on.

To our loyal clients—who over the years have trusted us to teach and guide your sales people in new ways of relating and selling to their female clients. We celebrate your successes!

To our readers—writing this book has been a great adventure. The concepts and tools have proven themselves over and over in countless organizations across the United States and Canada. We only hope you will embrace these concepts and apply their tools. As always, we're solidly on your side! We promise you'll produce spectacular results.

INTRODUCTION

First, We're on YOUR Side

We need to say right up front that we are biased. We are unabashedly on your side—the side of the salesperson. We know that for you to grow sales, you will have to win the hearts, minds, and pocket-books of women.

This is not another book on marketing to women or teaching women to become better-educated consumers. Unfortunately, in spite of all the snazzy ads, beautiful brochures, and slick media spots aimed at females, women are not always buying. They're shopping and leaving—taking their money with them.

This book is about selling. It's about actually closing sales to women clients—effectively, time after time. Our research over the past 15 years verifies that selling to women is a science that can be learned. We encourage you to try it. We offer proven, practical methods and tools in each chapter.

Second, the Gender Issue

As you read this book you may be tempted to believe that it was written only for men. Actually, it is written for sales professionals—both men and women. You will receive equal benefit, but in slightly different ways.

Today's sales professionals, men and women, have been immersed in traditional male-oriented sales approaches. Female sales people have been required to adopt traditional sales methods in order to "fit in." And though times are changing, business cultures around the world are still predominantly male.

If you are a man reading this book, you will undoubtedly recognize some typical male responses to a woman's behavioral style. You'll gain important insights into a woman's way of thinking, connecting, listening, decision-making, and timing. And by using these insights to shape your behavior you'll see amazing results in your ability to sell effectively to women.

If you are a woman reading this book, you may additionally find that you deeply understand how and why women buyers respond as they do. And you may find you've learned a sales approach that is sabotaging your own innate ability to relate effectively with your female clients. You may need to unlearn old approaches as well as learn new tools and techniques.

Either way, we believe you'll see yourself and many of your clients in the following examples and stories. As a sales professional, man or woman, we know that by practicing our approach, you will become RICH selling to women.

Now, For Men ONLY

Now that we've said that . . . we do have one chapter "for men only." It's the last chapter, and it's for all you men who want to take the learning to the next level—not only to increase your sales to women, but to build richer relationships with all of the wonderful women in your life.

Chapter 13 (yes, it's lucky!) will challenge you to translate your knowledge, skills, and techniques into a way of relating that will enhance your relationships for a lifetime. Enjoy the journey!

IT'S A WHOLE NEW BALL GAME

This book will show you how you can make more money than you have ever made before—by giving you the inside story on how to sell to a fast-growing and untapped market: women.

There are huge opportunities for selling to women out there, ripe for the plucking by anyone with the smarts to see them and the courage to try out new ways of selling.

Thanks to the impact of the women's movement, women who make up this market have been able to move beyond fighting discrimination and demanding equality. Today's women have the power, the money, and the confidence to insist on buying products and services in the ways that work best for *them*. If you can't do business the way they want, they'll find someone who can. No hard feelings. It's pretty much that simple.

The way most organizations are accustomed to selling is not in sync with the way most women want to buy.

Two converging trends have created this market.

Trend #1: Women are making more big-ticket purchases of traditionally male products

Women have moved beyond their traditional shopping venues. They now make big-ticket purchases of products and services— from building supplies to financial services to cars to electronics

INDUSTRIES WITH GROWING FEMALE CUSTOMER BASE

Financial planning / Stocks and bonds / Mortgages and equity loans / Banking services / Cars / Boats / Motorcycles / New houses / Building supplies / Furniture / Computers /Broadband, satellite, and cable systems / Security systems/ Heating and cooling systems / Insurance

to heating and cooling systems—once bought almost exclusively by men.

At some point in the last 5 years, women became the major purchasers and/or purchase influencers of traditionally male-oriented products. Why? It's no mystery: women started earning more money. Although women's salaries still average less than men's, today 48% of working wives provide at least half of the family income.

You may already know that women make or control 80% of all consumer buying decisions. But here are some statistics that might surprise you:

Women buy half of all sports equipment.

Women accounted for over half of the $96 billion spent on electronics in 2003.[1]

A third of all women consider themselves early adopters of cutting-edge technology.[2]

More single women than single men buy houses.

Women make up 48% of all investors in the stock market.[3]

Women's earnings have been increasing for some time. What's different now is that women have assets. Stocks and bonds. CD's. Rental property.

Trend #2: Women are embracing their D-gene

Remember when it was politically incorrect to imply that women and men were different in any but the most obvious

---

[1] Study by the Consumer Electronics Association quoted in "Consumer Electronics Companies Woo Women," AP January 15, May Wong.

[2] "Consumer Electronics Companies Woo Women"

[3] Chapter 13: Women and Finance, from WOW statistics, *Diversity Best Practices/ Business Women's Network,* Washington DC

WOMEN-OWNED BUSINESSES[4]

Between 1997 and 2002 the number of women- and equally-owned businesses jumped by 11%, versus 6% among all privately-held businesses.

The fastest growth rates are in the traditionally male industries: construction, agricultural services, transportation, communications and public utilities.

Today there are over 10.1 million women- or equally-owned businesses. They employ 18.2 million people, and earn revenues of $2.32 trillion in sales.

ways? When women in business wore suits and blouses with those floppy little bow ties? When they would never wear a dress to work for fear that people might think they were—well, female?

In those days, when "different" often got translated to mean "inferior," there were perfectly good reasons to downplay these distinctions.

Today, women have reached a point where they can not only admit to but appreciate and insist on their differences from men. And the more they do, the more they respond to products, services, and sales approaches that take these differences into account. In fact, so secure have women become about their differences from men that they can now laugh about them. Jokes about women get passed around the Internet—Did you hear about Buyagra? It's a stimulant taken prior to shopping that increases the duration and amount of spending. And it's often women who do the passing, and the laughing.

We refer to all the male–female differences, both the biological and the culturally acquired, as the D-gene. The D-gene refers to differences in how men and women communicate, how they relate to other people, how they make decisions, how they evaluate situations and how they buy.

[4] From National Women's Business Council, *Fact Sheet,* July 2003

In Chapter 3, "Decoding the D-Gene," we'll take a look at these differences. Although some are the product of social conditioning, you may be surprised to learn how many are genetic. Yes, now it can be told: men are hard-wired to be men, and women are hard-wired to be women.

The undecoded D-gene is often the reason some of life's charming little moments turn into great big ugly moments:

> - a woman's willingness to ask directions versus a man's insistence on finding his own way
> - a woman's interest in watching one TV show at a time versus a man's need to channel-surf
> - a woman's interest in going shopping versus a man's interest in making a purchase

We all recognize these potential flash points, although we don't all leverage them as creatively as the woman who was making a purchase in a department store. As she reached into her purse for her wallet, the salesperson noticed a remote control device.

"Do you always carry your TV remote with you?" the salesperson asked.

"No," she replied, "but my husband refused to come shopping with me, so I figured this was the worst thing I could to do him without getting arrested."

What gives this little story that ring of truth that makes us laugh? The D-gene.

Please understand: we're not claiming that one gender is better than the other. It's the D (for different) gene, remember, not the B (for better) gene. And we're certainly not saying that men don't try to bridge the gap. It's just that if you haven't decoded the D-gene, the gap can be virtually unbridgeable.

Take the man who was attending a marriage seminar with his wife. At one point the leader said that a good husband will always know his wife's favorite flower. Hearing this, the husband smiled, leaned over to his wife, gently touched her arm, and whispered proudly, "It's Pillsbury, isn't it?"

This guy is obviously sincere. He thinks he "got it," so what's the problem? Why the disconnect?

Right. It's the damned D-gene.

Even if you "get it," can you "do it"? The purpose of this book is to help you improve your sales to women, not your personal relationships, although we have found that one leads to the other. (More about that later.) We bring up these lighter moments because they illustrate at a domestic level the problem we find in sales organizations throughout North America.

Here's the situation; given the hugely expanded role women play in today's society, it's a surprising one:

By now, at the beginning of the twenty-first century, most organizations have made progress in reaching out to women—a little in some cases, a lot in others. Even organizations that sell traditionally male products have figured out how to make their marketing communications appeal to women. So, for example, we see an ad for a financial services company that shows two women talking about their investments over lunch.

Organizations are also making great strides in developing products designed with women in mind. One of the most exciting recent examples is Volvo's YCC (Your Concept Car), which was designed by and for women:

> ➤ The owner of a YCC will never have to lift the hood; in fact, you can't lift the hood. The car communicates with the dealership to check systems and schedule maintenance.

> ➤ Because women use the backseat for carrying packages more often than for passengers, the rear seats are folded up like theatre seats.

> ➤ Owners will be able to swap their seat covers and carpets whenever they want a new interior color scheme.

➤ There is even a function that determines if there is enough room in a parallel parking spot, and then helps steer the car into it.

It remains to be seen how many of these concept-car features make their way into Volvo's production models. What seems clear, however, is that we have come a long way from that 1955 lavender-and-pink Dodge with rosebud upholstery.

Given this progress, it is all the more remarkable that the way sales organizations sell to women has remained virtually unchanged, despite the changes of the last three decades. Companies still use pretty much the same spiel and the same techniques they did when most of their customers were men.

Whatever sensitivity about women's issues may exist in the executive suite or the marketing department doesn't always get to the sales force. This is puzzling, because in terms of customer impact, selling is where the rubber hits the road. Nevertheless, few salespeople know the specifics of how women like to go about making a purchase. Of those who do, fewer still can translate their awareness into effective female-focused selling behaviors.

Nowhere does an organization reveal its attitude toward women more vividly than in the behavior of its sales force.

There is a huge gulf between what we know we *should* do and our ability to actually do it, especially when the stakes are high. Take a look at any sport, and you'll see what we mean. Every golfer in the world knows you're supposed to keep your head down when you make a shot, right? So why don't they always do it?

Behavioral change isn't easy, and it doesn't happen overnight, especially when it involves something as ingrained as how we deal with the world as men, or as women. It's one thing for a company to "celebrate women," and put out female-focused marketing materials. It's another thing for a sales force to learn female-friendly selling behaviors thoroughly enough to use them consistently and effectively with women.

When we learn a new behavior, there is usually an old behavior we have to "unlearn." It takes courage to set aside old ways to try new approaches, especially when these old ways worked for us in the past. It also takes a willingness to practice, and a realization that to reach new levels of success you may have to go through a period of feeling a little awkward.

We are here to tell you that your opportunities for success with this new market are more than worth the effort. We believe that traditional male-oriented selling practices are the major stumbling block in an organization's attempt to engage successfully with women customers. Update your selling practices, and your future is unlimited.

WHAT THIS BOOK CAN DO FOR YOU

So here's the deal: the people who will get women's business will be those who take the trouble to decode the D-gene in the context of the product or service they sell, and adapt their behaviors accordingly. Using the concepts in this book, you will be able to create sales experiences for your women customers that are uniquely tailored to their needs and preferences.

We will tell you what most women won't—or can't:

> ➤ What women want at every point in a sales relationship
>
> ➤ What turns them off—immediately, and over time
>
> ➤ When to pursue, and when to back off
>
> ➤ How to encourage women to communicate their concerns directly to you
>
> ➤ How to read the subtle cues (surprisingly different from men's) that let you know how women are responding

Selling successfully to women does not require you to set aside everything you have ever learned about selling. You'll be able to stay within the guidelines of your existing selling process—although as you become more effective, you may find yourself using these concepts with all your customers, men as well as women.

Decoding the D-gene will pay off in several ways:

➤ Bigger and more sales to women

➤ Greater likelihood of successful cross-selling

➤ A higher conversion rate for your female prospects

➤ A growing group of loyal women customers—the kind who not only stick with you but also tell their friends about you

➤ More success with your male customers and prospects

and finally. . .

➤ An improvement in your relationships with the women in your life

Is this book for you? Check out the following chart and see for yourself:

Do you...	Then this book will...
1. Consider yourself already successfully selling to women?	Help you build on your success with some new tips and techniques.
2. Strive to treat male and female customers basically the same?	Increase your rate of success by showing you exactly how and under which circumstances women appreciate being treated differently.
3. Deal with your female customers by trying to be "softer" and avoiding statistics?	Demonstrate steps that create the difference between so-so results and get-rich success.
4. See women customers as mysteries; you never know where you stand with them, and are happy simply to avoid being offensive?	Give you the confidence to create successful sales strategies specifically designed with your women customers in mind.

| 5. Think most women suffer from male gender envy? | Challenge your thinking— enough, perhaps, to blast you out of your cave and into some successful sales to women. |

And remember, if you're a female salesperson, this book will give you permission to tap into your D-gene, and use it to make strong and profitable connections with your women customers.

A FINAL WORD

Throughout these pages you may take issue with some statements about the differences between men and women. "Wait a minute!" you might say. "I know plenty of women who don't behave—or think or feel—that way, and plenty of men who do!"

We do too. We recognize that all of us live on a continuum of human behavior with many areas of overlap and very few hard-and-fast divisions. Not all women like to shop, for example, just as not all men refuse to ask for directions. However, as general statements these differences describe most men and women, and we stand by them.

In the final analysis, of course, an effective salesperson needs to go beyond generalities to respond to each customer as a unique individual with a unique set of needs.

We believe that the insights and advice we offer here will help you do just that—move beyond the barriers of gender differences to establish profitable, long-term relationships with your female customers, customer by customer.

2 THE WOMEN'S MARKET FOR FINANCIAL SERVICES

Anyone who's been in the stock market during the late '90s and early part of this new century and claims not to have lost money is probably lying.

This may be a slight exaggeration, but it's no secret that the financial services industry is still climbing out of a hole. And although volumes have been written on who dug the hole, as far as bankers, brokers, and financial advisers are concerned, the result is a massive crisis in investor confidence. Many investors today are *still* waiting it out. According to one research firm, since the market crashed about $500 billion has moved from the equities markets to the sidelines, where it sits at banks as cash.[1]

> Having a trusting relationship with you is more important to a woman customer than knowing your performance record.

In the meantime, the structure of the market itself has changed. Commissions have been cut back. Thanks to the internet, individual investors can now conduct their research and do their investing on their own, without the aid of a professional. In other words, stocks and other investments have become commodities.

---

[1] Estimate by Celent Corp. in Boston, as quoted in "Firms Flaunt Transparency to Regain Investor Confidence," *Bank Technology News,* June 1, 2003.

The good news—there's got to be good news, right?—is that the way you restore investor confidence is also the way you tap into the billions and billions of investment dollars controlled by women: by developing and maintaining thoughtful, creative, honest, and proactive long-term relationships with your clients.

Yes, we know: everyone tries to develop relationships with his or her clients. The relationships we're talking about, however, are different from the kinds of relationships you may have with male customers: these are a little deeper, a little more "human," and a lot less cut-and-dried. They call for a new understanding and new behaviors. You'll probably need to pay a little more attention, be a little more creative, and share a lot more of yourself than you may be used to—not in a canned speech about the facts of your life ("Well, I'm married with two children, and I've been here 14 years, and . . ."), but in smaller moments that enable you to establish common ground and let her know the kind of a person you are ("I know what you mean. If a restaurant is too noisy, I don't care how good the food is.")

Is it worth the effort? Let's take a look at some facts and figures about women and money, and you can judge for yourself:

> Women represent 52% of the U.S. Population over age 18.[2]

> Women are projected to have 50% of U.S. private wealth by 2010. That's roughly $12.5 trillion. With a T.[3]

> 53% of working women own stocks and bonds. They represent 47% of all investors.[4]

> In 2002, 19.4 million single women owned their own homes.[5]

> Affluent women are younger than their male counterparts, which means that more of them are still working—

---

[2] U.S. Census Data 2002, Release Date June/2003.
[3] Conde Nast Publications.
[4] How to Get Rich Selling Cars to Women.
[5] Census Bureau's Marital Status and Living Arrangements: 2002.

and therefore have more time to build their wealth and increase their net worth.[6]

➤ Women head 40% of those households with assets of over $600,000.[7]

And finally. . .

➤ Women live an average of 5.4 years longer than men.[8]

Can you think of a reason to ignore a growing market with assets measured in the trillions of dollars?

STILL A MAN'S GAME

Before we go any further, there are a few things that need to be said about how women regard financial services. You probably won't hear them from your women customers, but if you want to be successful selling to women, these are things you need to know.

Please understand that we are not casting blame in any direction. The financial services industry has nothing to apologize for. Thanks in part to the innovative products it has developed over the years, private citizens at all income levels have been able to create personal assets that enhance their independence, improve their lives, and provide legacies for their children.

Nevertheless, most women—most people, actually—see the financial services industry as male-oriented, with male professional employees and male customers, and a corresponding masculine slant to its traditional business practices. We're going to tell you how you can adapt these practices to the D-gene, but first we need to talk about the power of the past, because it still

---

[6] A Business Proposal: High Net Worth Women: Capturing the Market.

[7] *How to Get Rich Selling Cars to Women*.

[8] *Ibid.*

exerts a strong influence on a woman's expectations and concerns when she walks in the door to do business with you.

When a woman works with a financial services professional, she probably feels, at some level, that she's playing a man's game. This is true even though:

> ➤ She may not lack self-esteem or the ability to assert her needs.

> ➤ She may be very wealthy and financially sophisticated, as more and more women are today.

> ➤ She may have a high-powered job.

> ➤ She may manage her own business and/or family finances.

> ➤ She may even be working with a woman broker or banker.

In the back of her mind there still lurks the feeling that she's operating in foreign territory. She may not even be aware of this feeling until something happens to trigger it.

To be successful with women, it's not enough to be good at your job. You also have to be good as a person.

That's what happened to Margaret, an executive with an outplacement firm. In her search for a new broker, she'd met once with Jeff, and was back for a second meeting to discuss his recommendations. Things were going well until he introduced her to Susan, his sales assistant. "He wasn't overtly rude to her," Margaret remembers. "It was just that old attitude of 'you're a woman, so you don't know what you're doing.' As Susan left the room, he even rolled his eyes at me, as if to say she didn't know what she was doing. That did it. I left and never returned. I realized the only reason he showed me any respect at all was because I had the money. But who knows what he would be saying behind my back?"

As a woman in a cigar shop, you may have gotten a taste of this feeling. As a man in the lingerie department, you may feel awkward and a little silly but it's different from feeling patronized.

Women have antennae that pick up all kinds of details. They will spot the slightest indication of condescending or patronizing behavior a mile away—even if you didn't intend it. And they can tell—as Margaret could with her broker—when the details don't add up.

A man on the receiving end of such treatment might not necessarily take it personally. A woman will. As a man you may find this reaction hard to understand. Perhaps you think the woman is being "over-sensitive"—but to succeed as a sales professional, you need to do everything in your power to avoid sending such signals.

WHAT YOUR WOMEN CUSTOMERS AREN'T TELLING YOU

If one of your women customers feels she is being discounted and tells you about it, consider yourself lucky. At least you know what the problem is, and stand a fighting chance of fixing it. More often, women who feel themselves treated badly will say nothing and simply leave—because they don't have the time to get into it, because they don't like to be confrontational, or because they figure that no matter what they say, you're a lost cause. But guess what? Even if they don't tell you, they'll tell twenty of their friends. (That's the power of female networking, and we'll tell you how you can put it to positive use later in the book.)

But what about the women who stay and say nothing? That must mean they're happy, right? Well, here are a couple of recent findings that shed new light on supposedly satisfied women customers:

> ➤ 84% of women in a Yankelovich survey said they felt misunderstood by investment professionals.[9]

---

[9] *Brand Notes* (newsletter), Vol. 1, Issue 110, May 2003.

> ➤ 55% of affluent women feel they are not taken as seriously by their financial advisers as men are.[10]

Although they shared this feeling with a researcher, they didn't share it with their investment professionals.

Why? Women are more relationship-oriented than men, and because of their cultural conditioning are less likely than men to rock the boat. Women are very experienced at adapting themselves to men; older women, especially, may not realize there's any other way—even in situations where they are the customers. The question is: how loyal are such women in these situations? Do you think they would stay with their financial adviser through thick and thin? Don't bet on it—not if a D-gene-savvy broker came along.

> *"My broker always asks me what he can do for me today. I no sooner start to answer than he's got a million suggestions."*

> *"If there is something in my account that can be improved, I think my personal banker should call me. Or is it only their new customers who get special treatment and better rates?"*

One woman we spoke to was a manager in her late 40s who had worked with a broker for over ten years. "He never really listened to me," she said. "He was just waiting for his chance to jump in and pontificate. I have to say, though, that he was good at the technical part of his job. Then a friend told me about *her* broker. She said he was a really good listener, and seemed to understand what she wanted.

"She set up a meeting for me, and I was really impressed. I suddenly realized that I didn't have to put up with being lectured at. Now I work with this new person, and I'm very happy."

As you'll see in the next chapter, women see a conversation with a broker or financial adviser in the context of a professional relationship in which the woman feels confident she can rely on her broker or financial adviser to do whatever is necessary to make her experience a positive one. This explains why, when

---

[10] *She Said.* Study conducted by Maddox Smye, Deloitte, Yankelovich Partners, 1998.

asked to describe positive experiences with a financial services provider, women mentioned examples of service six times more frequently than examples of financial performance or success.[11]

So what *don't* women like about their brokers? Here's a list of quotes that come directly from our interviews with the women customers of bankers and brokers:

> ➤ *He doesn't listen.* "I can tell the minute his attention wanders. You know, I get enough glazed-eye listening from my husband at the dinner table. From my broker I expect better."

> ➤ *He monopolizes the conversation.* "My banker asks me questions but can't seem to stop talking long enough for me to answer."

> ➤ *She doesn't take my calls.* "My broker doesn't answer my calls any more. I'm sure it's because she pulls up my account and sees how much money I've lost, and assumes I'm calling to complain. But if she doesn't start taking my calls, she's going to lose an easy account."

> ➤ *He assumes my husband has the final word.* "Our broker would call and pitch an investment to me. When I agreed to buy, he'd say, 'Is this something you and your husband *both* want?' We don't get any more of these insulting calls, because we moved our account."

> ➤ *She's not warm or outgoing.* "The atmosphere in my bank is so chilly. Do they all hate their jobs? I would never move my investment accounts there."

> ➤ *He treats me impersonally.* "I took my money from a brokerage firm to a bank, because I felt the brokerage was not personal; it seemed like they used the same formula on everyone. When I told this to my new banker, she gave me her home phone number and said to call any time, day or night."

[11] *She Said*

➤ *She rushes me.* "I always get the impression that if I don't act right away, I'll lose out. I can't make decisions under that kind of pressure. Besides, I think it's my broker who's worries about losing out—on a quick commission."

➤ *He wastes my time.* "I had scheduled an appointment with my broker during my son's band practice. So I dropped off my son, dashed to the broker's office, and sat there waiting for twenty minutes. That cut my time with him almost in half, because I still had to pick up my son. What the broker didn't understand was that I have no time in my day to sit and wait—and if I did, it wouldn't be in his office."

➤ *He brags.* "I'm not saying he's lying; I know he's good. But whenever he starts tooting his own horn, I turn off. Is he so insecure that he thinks he needs to do that?"

WHAT SOME BROKERS SAY ABOUT THE CHALLENGES OF WORKING WITH WOMEN CUSTOMERS

If that's what women have to say about their bankers and brokers, what do sales professionals have to say about their women customers? Here are some typical comments:

➤ *I never know where I stand with them.* "If I make a presentation to a guy, and he doesn't buy, I figure, 'Oh well, win some, lose some.' With a woman, I always wonder, 'Did I do something wrong? Did I offend her in some way?'"

➤ *They pay more attention to their hairdresser than they do to me.* "I've got a customer with a whole network of 'advisers.' I make a recommendation, and the next week she asks six different people about it, and of course she gets six different opinions. My advice doesn't seem to count for any more than her unemployed brother-in-law's."

> *They tell me their life stories.* "I mean, OK, their grandson is cute. But then they tell me about their son and his wife and their problems, and on and on and on. I really am willing to listen. The problem is, I've scheduled an hour for our meeting, and by the end of the hour nothing has happened."

> *They ask too many questions.* "Women can get so intense. The more I tell them, the more they ask me. It's like they're trying to cover any possible eventuality. Some of that's a good thing, but 'lighten up,' is what I say."

> *They take too long to make decisions.* "I'll call her—you know, check in to see where she is. But I get the feeling she doesn't want to be pressured, so now I don't know how to move things along. We could both be dead before she closes."

WOMEN ARE INCLINED TO INVEST

> *93% of women fear not having enough money in their old age.*

> *77% want financial independence*

> *80% did research and planning before purchasing securities*

> *72% choose conservatively, low risk and return*

THE IRONY OF THE SITUATION

If you look at what the brokers and bankers say, it's all about the fact that women don't fit into the traditional way brokers and bankers do business. Women take "too long," talk "too much," and ask "too many" questions.

Women's complaints, on the other hand, center around the lack of a personal relationship. Brokers and bankers don't listen. They're not friendly. They treat clients impersonally. They don't return calls.

The irony is that, despite all their complaints, research demonstrates that women are more disposed than men to listen to their financial advisers:

> ➤ More women than men regard their financial adviser as their prime source of financial advice (36% of women, 26% of men). Men are twice as likely to rely on newspapers, newsletters, and magazines (23%) as women (12%).[12]

> ➤ 90% of women look to their financial advisers to teach as well as advise them. Only 75% of men feel this way.[13]

> ➤ Working-age women are more likely to consult a financial professional when investing (62%) than men (less than 50%).[14]

> ➤ Women are more loyal than men. Once a woman feels she can trust her broker, she'll stay with him. A man, on the other hand, is more focused on a broker's performance. If the performance drops, the man is likely to move on.

If, as a broker or banker, you want to tap into the enormous women's market, the message is clear: you need to spend at least as much time establishing trusting relationships with your women customers as you do developing your market knowledge and technical expertise. The secret lies in your ability to adapt what you do to the needs and preferences of your women customers throughout a sale— from the critical initial minutes of a first meeting to the sale's close; from service and support after the sale to maintaining an ongoing relationship with your customer that will produce additional leads and sales in the future.

And how do you do this? The first step is learning how to decode the D-gene. That's the topic of the next chapter.

[12] *Time*, May 22, 2002.

[13] *Oppenheimer Funds Survey*.

[14] *Women's Retirement Confidence Survey,* Mathew Greenwell & Associates & Employee Benefit Research Institute, 1999.

DECODING THE D-GENE

What are the differences between men and women—and why should you care about them? So far we've been talking about the D-gene in general terms. Now it's time to get specific.

In this chapter we will concentrate on the four areas of male–female differences that have the greatest impact on the buying (and therefore the selling) process:

> How men and women relate to other people

> How they express themselves

> How they take in and process information

> How they make decisions

This is the information you need to maximize your sales to women. It can mean the difference between striking out (or making a one-time sale) and creating loyal customers who trust you to do what's best for them over the long haul.

WHERE DO THE DIFFERENCES COME FROM?

Are women different from men because of their genetic make-up or because of how they were raised? There's no simple answer to this nature–nurture debate—although recent research seems to be swinging the pendulum toward nature. In other words, you can forbid your young son to play with toy guns, but don't be

> ### BLAME IT ON THE D-GENE #2
>
> *Why do women always have the last word?*
>
> *Because anything a man says after that becomes the beginning of the next argument.*

surprised if he chews a piece of toast into the shape of a pistol and starts firing away.

We are all products of our evolution. The male–female differences that developed many thousands of years ago to ensure the perpetuation of our species live on in each of us, even though we no longer need them to survive and they no longer limit the roles we play. Everyone knows that women today can be bread-winners, and men can stay home and raise children. Et cetera.

Nevertheless, some significant male–female differences remain, stronger in some individuals than in others. They are at the root of the tension between the sexes that people often defuse through humor (see the "Blame it on the D-gene" boxes in this chapter). When it comes to selling successfully to women, however, these differences deliver more than a few laughs. Once you understand them, you have the keys to the kingdom.

Our purpose here is to help you increase your sales. It would be a mistake at this point to veer off into an argument over which differences are "better." There is no "better" or "worse," there is only "different." The only point we want to make is that a salesperson can use this understanding to accommodate him or herself to the preferences of women customers—and as a result achieve greater success in terms of initial sales, loyal customers, repeat business, and referrals.

Any discussion of the D-gene has got to start with *hormones* (don't worry: this is not a biology lecture). Most people know that testosterone is the male hormone, and estrogen the primary female hormone—although women have some testosterone, and men have some estrogen.

> ➤ Testosterone is what makes men strong, competitive, aggressive, and inclined to take risks. Research tells us that testosterone also contributes to such other traits as math and analytical ability, mechanical skills, and a talent

for navigating and reading maps. (There is no indication that it facilitates operation of a television remote control.) These qualities were vital in the days when men had to compete for and keep mates, hunt for food, and protect their families against danger.

> Estrogen is the female equivalent of testosterone. It increases a woman's interest in nest-building and nurturing. Another hormone, progesterone, triggers the maternal feelings she needs to bond with her infant. Oxytocin, which helps induce labor, also facilitates mother-and-child bonding. In fact, during some moments of stress, when

RELATIONSHIP-ORIENTED FROM THE GET-GO

Female infants sustain eye contact twice as long as boys. They're also better at distinguishing between photos of people they know and people they don't.

men release the adrenaline that produces the "fight or flight" syndrome, women release oxytocin, which drives them to seek safety and solace with others, a response that is sometimes referred to as "tend and befriend." In fact, researchers now believe oxytocin helps women form healthy interpersonal relationships of all kinds.

> Researchers also believe that women's higher levels of the hormone seratonin reduce their aggression and interest in risk-taking activities.

A woman's interest in forming emotional connections with other people is permanent and deep-seated. This is why it's so important to establish a trustworthy relationship with your woman customers, and why they are not motivated by the competition that drives many sales to men.

THE FEMALE BRAIN

A woman's brain is indeed wired differently from a man's. Men's brains tend to have clearly separated functions. Women's brains, by and large, tend to have more internal connections, within and across hemispheres. Women's emotional centers, for example, are found in many parts of the brain, while men's are concentrated in the right side. This interconnected distribution may support a broader, more nonlinear thinking style in women, in contrast to a man's more focused approach.

> **BLAME IT ON THE D-GENE #3**
>
> *A successful **man** is one who makes more money than his wife can spend.*
>
> *A successful **woman** is one who can find such a man.*

This difference is good to keep in mind while you listen to a woman tell you what her financial needs are. Instead of trying to control your impatience with her "rambling," if you can instead tune into her different style of thinking, you'll find you can listen attentively and with respect. The payoff for you: you'll gain valuable information—and you'll earn her loyalty.

EXPECTATIONS OF SOCIETY

Although the gap between the rules for males and females has certainly narrowed in the last forty years, there is still plenty of social pressure on women and girls to be quiet, compliant, and "polite," and not to get angry or interrupt others.

As a salesperson, therefore, you need to make sure you don't unwittingly play into these pressures by making her "fight" to get her point across. You need to avoid assuming that her compliance equals agreement and encourage (but not pressure) her to speak up.

THE D-GENE AND SELLING TO WOMEN

With this quick background, let's return to the four sales-related areas where the D-gene has the biggest impact, and take a look at what you can do to accommodate your sales approach to how women like to buy.

As you read, think about your company's current sales process, and how you sell now. Is the way you sell a male-oriented approach? Is it tailored primarily to men? Do you see places where you can modify your approach to respond to women's preferences?

Again, keep in mind that we are talking about *most* men and *most* women. Don't get hung up on the people you may know who behave differently. Once you get the overall model, you can modify your approach to people who exhibit a combination of male and female characteristics.

1. How men and women relate to other people

Men see themselves as independent operators who relate to others by achieving goals and solving problems; there is often a strong element of competition involved. Women see themselves in terms of their relationships, and relate to others by sharing and establishing emotional connections. For example:

Women	Men
Woman are relationship-oriented. They derive identity from their place in relationships.	Men are transaction-oriented; they derive identity from what they do and achieve.
Women are conditioned to get along, be nice. They work to ensure win/win outcomes. They like to share, equalize, work together. They see themselves as part of a culture of equals.	Men are raised on and comfortable with competition and win/lose outcomes. A man sees himself as part of a hierarchy, with some people above and some below him. Men are more comfortable in a command-and-control environment.

Women	Men
Women thrive on courtesy and respect. Politeness and manners, insofar as they build bridges and avoid conflict, mean a lot to them. The closer competition gets to overt conflict, the more uncomfortable women become with it.	Men thrive on competition. They see negotiation as a challenging game in which they can test their skills and perhaps dominate the other person. Their physical contact with other men is often rough and jostling.
A woman's style is to create community, brainstorm with others, build consensus.	A man's style is to dominate, interrupt, give advice, and do more telling than asking.
Women tend to be open to the input and influence of others.	Men resist being influenced by others; they prefer to be seen as making up their own minds.

SELLING TIPS

Whatever you can do to establish and maintain a relationship with a woman customer will make her feel more comfortable and therefore more likely to buy from you. Establishing such a connection should be your primary goal; if you do that, the sale will almost take care of itself.

> **BLAME IT ON THE D-GENE #5**
>
> *"Of course we talk more than men," one woman said. "We have to say everything twice because men don't listen."*

➤ One way to build a relationship is to find commonalities in your lives—children, hobbies, favorite authors, travel—and share them. Remember to ask about them whenever you talk.

➤ Look for times when you can share your feelings. That's right: feelings. Let's face it: you'll never create a strong personal bond by discussing price/earnings ratios. The more you open up, the more she'll trust you. Don't be afraid to ask about her thoughts and feelings, either.

> Introduce her to "your team"—the people in your office who are involved in servicing her account. Make the point that these people are also "her team," And that they are very important to you.

> Host gatherings that bring together your women customers and/or prospects. Make sure these events are small enough for people to get to know each other.

2. How men and women express themselves

This just in: women talk more than men. In one study women clocked in at 25,000 words a day (versus 12,000 for men). As a man, you may think women talk primarily to transmit information. Wrong. That's what *men* do. Women also talk to connect, to check on and maintain relationships, to find their place in a group, and to feel safe. For example:

Women	Men
Women like communication with more context, emotional content, and detail. They tend to tell the whole story, starting at the beginning.	Men like communication that is concise, streamlined, and often focused on specific actions or results.
Women value communication as a way to interact, express emotions and offer intuitions.	Men value communication as a way to give and receive information, discover and express facts.
Women talk more often in terms of preferences and suggestions. They ask more question than men.	Men talk more often in terms of information and advice. They ask fewer questions.

Women	Men
Women's language is characterized by disclaimers ("I'm no expert, but…") and qualifiers ("Don't you think we should…"). They make fewer direct statements than men.	Men's language is more direct, with fewer qualifiers than women. It's also characterized by teasing, joking, and verbal bantering.
Women tend to disclose personal information about themselves as part of establishing connections with others.	Men tend not to disclose personal information. It's their way of protecting their independence, and keeping their options open.
Women make eye contact while talking with another person.	Men make less eye contact while talking with others.
Women interrupt less. They also allow more interruptions, although they don't like being interrupted.	Men interrupt more, and allow fewer interruptions.

SELLING TIPS

> Don't waste your time trying to cut a woman off, or hurry her story along. She won't like it, and besides, you can't do it. The fact is, if you know how to listen, everything a woman says is golden. If you pay attention to what she says, you'll eventually be able to offer products and services that fit perfectly into her life—including some she may not even know she needs.

> Don't assume that just because she doesn't always "cut to the chase," she doesn't know what she wants. A woman may soften assertions with various qualifiers—"That's awfully expensive, isn't it?"—but don't assume she's not serious or well-informed.

> Maintain eye contact. If you're a man, this might feel awkward at first; when men talk, they tend not to look at each

other as much as women do. To a woman, not looking her in the eye makes you seem shifty and untrustworthy.

> Don't interrupt. Or, to put it another way: DON'T INTERRUPT! For men, interrupting or being interrupted is part of the normal give-and-take of a conversation. The better the conversation, the more the interruptions. Not so for a woman. Women wait their turn. Nothing makes a woman feel more irritated or discounted than being interrupted. You may know where her conversation is heading. You may know exactly what she needs. You may have an exciting idea you just can't wait to present. Forget about it. Bite your tongue until it's bloody, if you need to, but . . . don't interrupt.

BLAME IT ON THE D-GENE #4

Men at lunch: *When a bill for $52.50 arrives, each of the four guys will throw in a twenty. None will have anything smaller—and no one will admit to wanting any change back.*

Women at lunch: *When the bill arrives, out come the pocket calculators.*

3. How men and women take in and process information

Think of a funnel with information going in the top and coming out the bottom. With a woman, the funnel stays wider longer and takes in a greater variety of information. With a man, it narrows sooner, discarding "extraneous" data along the way. For example:

Women	Men
Women see themselves as students. They're comfortable asking for help and admitting what they don't know.	Men see themselves as masters of a situation. They're less comfortable asking for help and admitting what they don't know.

Women	Men
Women think more concretely, often organizing information into stories.	Men think more abstractly. They look for principles, rules, patterns.
When applying the rules, women are often more interested in the person's circumstances than in an abstract notion of good and bad. They use their own experiences and examples to make decisions.	Men often see situations in abstract terms of right and wrong, good and bad. They are more likely than women to think that the rules should be applied equally to everyone.
Women listen actively and physically —nodding, smiling, gesturing.	Men listen passively. Often they show little or no response at all.
Women nod to indicate they are listening.	Men nod to indicate agreement.
Women are more sensitive than men to body language, emotional states, and nonverbal cues.	Men tend to focus on the objective facts.
Women seek to expand their perspective and search out options.	Men tend to analyze, sifting through facts to eliminate those that don't apply so they can zero in on the key points.

SELLING TIPS

> ➤ Do less lecturing. With women disposed to listen and ask questions, and men disposed to see themselves as experts, the temptation to pontificate can be powerful. Resist it at all costs.

> ➤ Tell more stories when you talk about your products. Include your customer in them—her goals, her needs, her family, her future.

> ➤ LISTEN. This, of course, is the flip side of NO INTERRUPTING.
> ➤ *Show* that you're listening. Nod, say "mm-hm," inject a response from time to time to let her know you're tracking. Remember, a woman can usually spot someone who is only pretending to listen.

4. How men and women make buying decisions

For a woman, making a purchase in a traditionally male industry will almost always be a high-stakes decision, regardless of the cost of the product. Along with her lack of experience in the area, and a concern that she may be taken advantage of, she does not want to get home and have her husband or boyfriend say, "They really sold you a bill of goods! How much did you pay⁈" For example:

BLAME IT ON THE D-GENE #6

A woman asks her husband to help her shop for a dress for an upcoming cocktail party. "I was thinking of something red," she says.

As soon as they get to the store, he spots a red dress on the rack and says, "This looks nice. Why don't you try it on?"

When she comes out of the dressing room, she looks really great and he tells her so.

She agrees—which is why he's surprised when she insists they check out what other stores have to offer.

And at the end of the day, which dress does she buy? Right, the one they saw first.

What the husband thinks they did: waste their time.

What the wife thinks they did: research.

Women	Men
Women feel a need to make the "perfect" or "right" decision.	Men are generally satisfied with a "good" decision.
Women tend to buy a relationship. They are influenced by how they're treated.	Men tend to buy a product. They are influenced by the deal they got.
A woman often begins the buying process by talking with others she knows who are knowledgeable.	Men tend to begin the process with independent research.

Women	Men
A woman's buying process encompasses a circular search pattern, involving thinking, discussing, comparing, and collaborating. For her, a purchase is about the process.	A man's buying process is more linear—from research to the purchase. For him, it's about solving a problem.
Women express interest in what a product or service does for them and for those who matter to them.	Men express interest in a product's or service's efficiencies, and how it works.
Women take longer to decide, but in the end are more loyal customers.	Men make quicker decisions, but are fickle and less loyal.

SELLING TIPS

> Be patient. Don't indicate in any way that she's taking too long to make up her mind. (And don't forget that women are experts at reading body language.)

> Prepare yourself for second (and third and fourth) opinions. A woman may seek advice from everyone she knows—and when it comes to financial services, you can be sure they will each have their two cents to add. You may be irritated at having your advice equated with your customer's hairdresser's, but there isn't much you can do about it.

> Keep the relationship uppermost in your mind—because she certainly will. You may have put together a stellar long-term financial plan for her, but if you don't return her calls promptly, she may not return yours—ever.

> Help her connect emotionally with the product by showing how it will make her life better, as well as the lives of those she cares about.

Now that you know about the D-gene and what it is telling you, you're ready to apply your new knowledge to the fine-tuning of your overall selling approach.

NOT UNTIL SHE TRUSTS YOU

What Women Want Most in a Buying Experience

Research tells us that when it comes to making large purchases, men look first for value—the deal they're able to get. Next comes the salesperson's likeability, and finally his or her trustworthiness.

With women, it's exactly the opposite. Before anything else, a woman needs to trust the salesperson she's working with, especially in a traditional male industry. Then comes likeability, and then value. (Women tend to see value emerging from the relationship.) She is looking for clues she can trust you the minute she walks in the door. (See Chapter 5, "The Two-Minute Take-Off.") If trust is not there, the game is over before it begins, as far as the woman is concerned.

What a woman seeks in a caring relationship with her banker, broker or financial adviser is a little different from what a man looks for. Both, obviously, want to know that you will live up to your word, and that you have their best interests at heart. A woman, however, has some additional requirements:

> *"I could not trust the broker I was working with. He kept wanting me to invest more money—but I never understood what he sent me or what he told me."*

- ➤ Can she rely on the strength of a personal relationship with you?

- ➤ Can she trust you as an ally to understand the pressures in her life and help her ease them?

➤ Can she rely on getting special treatment from you, if she needs it—not because she is a special person (or not *only* because she is a special person), but because she may be short of time and experience?

TRUST IS A FUNNY THING

Trust is a much-valued but often misunderstood quality. You demonstrate your trustworthiness over time, not all at once. Ultimately, it's up to other people to decide whether you're trustworthy or not.

Here are a few more things you need to know about trust:

➤ People make their decisions by carefully evaluating your behavior—not so much the grand gestures as how you behave in the smaller moments. That's why it takes a long time for trust to grow.

> **WHAT ABOUT MEN?**
>
> *Don't men like special treatment, too? Sure they do. But for women it plays a bigger part in a satisfying buying experience.*

➤ Once someone trusts you, they no longer need further proof of your trustworthiness. They will then take your word, follow your advice, and accept your recommendations.

➤ However—and it's a BIG however—it takes only a moment to break this trust, and a long, long time to earn it back.

THE 5 PRINCIPLES OF TRUST-BASED SELLING

We've organized into five principles everything you need to do to engender trust in your women customers:

Think relationship before product.

Respect her, her time, and her timing.

Understand her on her own terms.

Surpass her every expectation.

Telegraph confidence.

If you can internalize these principles and use them to shape your behavior, you'll have customers who will be open to your advice, stay with you through good times and bad, and tell so many of their friends how wonderful you are that you'll never have to make another cold call.

1. Think relationship before product

Because a woman relates more to people than to things, she finds it easier to connect with you than with the product you're selling. To her, the sales relationship comes before the sale. Whereas a man is looking for the best deal, a woman is looking for a total buying experience. You'll earn her trust (and her business) if you take the time to invest in getting to know her and letting her get to know you. There will be plenty of time to share your extensive product knowledge once you've established a connection. So slow down. Don't try to shoe-horn her into the timeframe that would work for a man.

WHAT THIS MEANS FOR YOU

If you can pace yourself to accommodate her process, you'll avoid frustration—and she'll relax and begin to feel more comfortable doing business with you.

HOW TO BRIDGE THE D-GENE

The challenge for most salespeople—men and women alike—is to shift their initial focus away from what they're selling. Although they may understand the importance of establishing a relationship with their customers, most salespeople do not realize just how "human" women customers need this relationship to be.

> *Allow time for her to get to know you—and you to get to know her.* When you're selling to a woman, expect a process rather than an event. Think of it as a trip from Point A to Point B: a man gets on an eight-lane interstate and is there in three hours. A woman takes the back roads and doesn't arrive for two days. That's because the woman wants to experience the trip itself so she can get comfortable with the new territory.

> You can't speed up her journey, so put it out of your mind. In the first place, if you spend all your time wishing she'd get on the interstate, as a woman she's going to pick up the vibe that you're rushing her, even if you don't say anything. Secondly, you're going to lose out on the chance not only to build a strong relationship, but to learn things about her that will help you know what products or services to recommend.

THIS OLD THING?

With greater powers of observation, you may even wise up to your spouse's habit of slipping new clothes past you. You know the one: "New? Oh no, honey, I've had this dress for ages."

> *Establish common ground.* This is different from the male practice of checking each other out to see who went to the better college, earns the higher salary, or drives the faster car. With women, the point is to find commonalities that will help bring them together as equals.

> Check to see what pastimes you share. Bring up community events she may have attended. See what she thinks of the new restaurant in town.

Don't be afraid to ask questions, but make sure you're not interrogating her. Lead with personal information of your own, and see if she responds. Pets and children (or grandchildren) resonate with almost everyone.

➤ *Notice what she may be carrying with her.* It could be a picture on a key chain, a travel brochure, or children's book. Use it to create a connection: "I couldn't help noticing the picture you have on your keychain. You must be a cat lover, too."

The key here is to be observant. With the exception of people like Sherlock Holmes and Lt. Columbo, men aren't known for having an abundance of this trait—but with practice you'll be surprised how much you can pick up.

➤ *Remember her name and the names of the significant people in her life.* This may sound obvious, but it's especially important to women. If Julie calls you for some information, and you call her Jenny, she probably won't hang up on you, but you will have definitely lost some ground in earning her trust. On the other hand, if you can refer to her son or grandson by name, she will certainly think, and may even say, "Oh, you remembered!"

➤ *Act as her ally in the sales process.* Think of your organization's sales process. Where are the potential bottlenecks? Where's the red tape? Where are problems likely to arise? Remember, she's a busy person, and will appreciate anything you can do to help expedite the process for her. So don't just hand her over to the back office when you've closed the sale. Introduce her to the people she'll be working with. Help her understand the papers she must sign. Intercede on her behalf if a problem

DEMON MULTI-TASKERS

*In the same time it takes the **husband** to make the morning coffee, the **wife** will fix breakfast, pack the kids' lunches, write a shopping list, iron a shirt, call the office, find missing homework, and de-flea the cat.*

crops up. If she's looking for a special arrangement, or an exception to one of your rules, see what you can do to accommodate her. Your efforts will pay off in her trust—and in future sales from her and her friends.

2. Respect her, her time, and her timing

You can respect a woman customer, first of all, by treating her with courtesy—not only the pull-her-chair-out-from-the-table kind but also the respectful deference that tells her she's the focus of your efforts. Second, you will never go wrong if you can always remember how short of time she is. By and large, women are a lot busier than men, especially working women. Women, with their ability to multi-task, are often given multiple responsibilities to juggle at work. And at home? Well, married working women still shoulder the bulk of family responsibilities. And being a single mom is not exactly a walk in the park.

> **TIME IS PRECIOUS TO WOMEN**
>
> ➤ 63% of working women spend 40 hours or more on the job.
> ➤ 40% of women 25 to 54 years old report that they have less than one hour a day for themselves.

WHAT THIS MEANS FOR YOU

Because it's so important for women to feel they're being taken seriously, you can set yourself apart by going out of your way to extend respect. Quiet, focused forms of attention register big with women.

If you can support whatever decision-making approach your woman customer wants to use—asking lots of questions, conferring with friends and family members, taking her time—you'll earn her respect, gratitude, and future business.

HOW TO BRIDGE THE D-GENE

Your biggest challenge as a sales professional may be dealing with a woman's time pressures on the one hand, and, on the other, the time she needs to make a decision. To you, it might seem that the solution would be to help her decide faster. Here's a more effective approach:

> *Learn about her schedule and timeframe for making decisions.* When you're five or ten minutes late for a meeting with a male customer, it's not good—but it's not the end of the world. A woman, on the other hand, may have planned her day so closely that she can't afford to lose this time. She may be paying a dollar for every minute she's late picking up her kid at child care. More important for your future relationship with her, a woman is much more likely than a man to take your lateness personally—as if you didn't respect her enough to make an effort to be on time.

> *Let your woman customer set the pace each step of the way.* When you check with the woman before proceeding to the next step, you're showing respect by putting her in charge of the conversation.

Make a conscious effort to say things that put the woman in charge, such as "Is that something you'd like to get into today?" or "When you're ready, I'd be happy to go over that with you."

Avoid phrases like, "In order to save time, I'd like to. . . ." "We need to make a decision soon so we don't lose out on this opportunity," or "Let's move on to the next point." And never look at your watch, unless it's to hurry yourself along.

> **TURN OFF YOUR PHONE**
>
> *One woman we spoke to loves the fact that her broker always closes the door and turns off his phone when she's in his office.*
>
> *"I like the feeling that I don't have to compete for his attention," she says.*

> **THE ULTIMATE SACRIFICE?**
>
> *Letting the woman set the pace of the conversation is the equivalent of giving her the remote control.*

Instead of saying "I hate to rush you, but I have another appointment," put the onus on yourself: "It looks like I haven't scheduled enough time for our meeting. Would you like to set up another one?"

> *Use your manners.* It's very simple: a lack of courtesy is a deal-breaker with women. So dust off your manners. And remember that women will notice how you treat other people. One woman reported having lunch with her banker, whom she observed taking a high-handed tone with the waiter. "It made me think less of her," she said.

Because a woman may be more sensitive to being snubbed or excluded, avoid humor or topics of conversation she might not care about or be offended by.

Wait to use nicknames until she invites you to. You don't want to run the risk of seeming pushy. (In this regard, you'll probably want to ask rather than assume that your relationship is on a first-name basis.)

3. *Understand her on her own terms*

For a woman, the goal of a conversation is to understand and to be understood as a person, not just in business terms. The point is not simply to trade information or establish dominance, as it often is for men.

As the D-gene tells us, women's natural ways of speaking and listening are different from men's. Women tend to avoid black-or-white statements. They use more qualifiers and disclaimers, in an effort to invite the other person into the conversation. Women also use more questions and upward inflections in order to see if the other person is in step with them.

Women expect to take turns when they talk, without having to fight to be heard. At times, women may appear hesitant or timid in conversation. In point of fact, these pauses are quite functional. Women are merely waiting to hear your response—and they would like you to do the same.

WHAT THIS MEANS FOR YOU

If you can modify your own conversational style to sync up with your women customers', you'll be letting them know that you're taking them seriously and tracking with them on both a business and more interpersonal level. If you can enter her world by being respectful of—and responsive to—her preferred conversational style, you'll get insights into her needs and decision-making rationale you could never otherwise hope for. For a salesperson, this is golden information.

HOW TO BRIDGE THE D-GENE

Don't be surprised if this principle proves challenging. Women's and men's conversational styles—in fact, the dynamics of their interactions—are very different, as you saw in the last chapter. Men listen differently from women. They react much less. The first time we ever gave a presentation to an all-male audience, we thought we were bombing. They just sat there. Afterward, they had lots of questions and comments; it was obvious that they had been listening closely, but it didn't look that way to us. When we talk to groups of women, on the other hand, it can feel as if the building is about to take off. They smile, they nod, they gesture, they make comments to their friends. It's . . . well, it's different.

Historically, women have pushed for more and better service—like stores staying open 24/7, for example. Once in place, however, these improvements appealed as much to men as they did to women.

➤ *Value her conversation style.* Expect it to be more detailed and descriptive than what you will hear from men. If you can stop trying to "net out" what she's saying, or get her to "cut to the chase," you'll learn a lot about who she is. And what salesperson doesn't need to know more about his or her customers?

➤ *Over-respond!* If women don't get frequent responses, they will assume you're not listening. So over-respond; it may feel forced at first, but you'll get used to it, and she'll get the picture that you're paying attention. By over-respond, we mean nodding, maintaining eye contact, dropping in some uh-huhs and I sees, asking questions to learn more ("What was that like for you?"), and reflecting back her feelings ("You sound angry. I'd feel the same way if I were in your position.") We'll have more to say on this topic in Chapter 6.

➤ *Pay attention.* It bears repeating that a woman hates to talk to a man who is pretending to listen. You think women don't know that blank look when they see it? Think again. If you want to establish trusting relationships with your women customers, you may to need to come up with some strategies for tuning in. One man reported he pretended he'd be quizzed on everything his customer was telling him.

➤ *Resist the temptation to interrupt.* We said it before and we'll say it again: Never interrupt. This a huge mistake on several levels: (1) it's rude, (2) it indicates you're not taking her seriously, (3) it increases her anxiety by making her feel she must compete to be heard, and (4) you're cutting her off from saying things that could be useful to you.

4. Surpass her every expectation

Although men certainly appreciate service above and beyond the call of duty, by and large your efforts to exceed expectations will have a bigger impact on women. It makes them feel special, it tells them you value the relationship, and it gives them the comfortable feeling that they are being well taken care of. Finally, there's no better way to set yourself apart—and above—your competition.

There are two parts to this principle: first, the extra help you provide to make sure transactions go as smoothly as possible for her, and second, your thoughtful gestures that underscore the importance to you of the relationship.

> When it comes to helping their customers, financial advisers can find themselves involved in everything from arranging car leases to sorting through a dead relative's financial records.

WHAT THIS MEANS FOR YOU

Women have exceptional memories, and they like to share with other people. If you are able to do more for them than you promised—provide them with small extras even before they can think to ask for them—they'll reward you with their business, and also recommend you to their friends.

HOW TO BRIDGE THE D-GENE

The dual challenge for most salepeople is to remember how important this principle is for their women customers, and to be as creative as possible in going that extra mile. It's not about sending flowers or making the grand gesture. It's about knowing enough about her to do just the thing that will make her life a little happier and more hassle-free. In other words, this is where all that listening you've been doing can really pay off.

➤ *Attend to the details.* Making an effort to become more detailed-oriented can really pay off. If you call a client to make an appointment, and you're able to say, "I know Wednesday afternoons are out, because that's when you volunteer at the Garden Center. How about Thursday?" she'll appreciate the fact that you remembered her schedule.

If you have a hard time even remembering your own wedding anniversary, you may want to think about getting some help. Is there someone in your office who can make sure you keep track of things? An electronic tickler file you could set up?

➤ *Under-promise and over-deliver.* It's always safer to take the conservative path. In the first place, a woman doesn't like people who toot their own horns, and if you make outlandish promises, that's what she'll think. Secondly, when you can't deliver, you not only disappoint her, you add seeds of doubt about just how important she is to you, and how trustworthy you are overall. So if the check won't come for two weeks, tell her that—and then do whatever you can to get it there faster.

➤ *Do everything you can to make her life easier.* If something has gone wrong for her, step in and fix it. If the screw-up is somewhere in your own organization, find out who's responsible. Follow up, and let her know what you're doing. (We'll have more to say about this in Chapter 9.)

➤ *Surprise her with unexpected human gestures.* How about keeping some cookies on hand to go with the coffee? A jar of hard candy? Send her a newspaper clipping that relates to something she told you. You're letting her know that she's important enough for you to have listened—and remembered. When you send a greeting card or follow-up note, do you use the company stationery, or do you take the trouble to pick out a nice card you think she would like? (We'll explore this topic in much greater detail in Chapter 10.)

5. *Telegraph confidence*

A woman wants a qualified and reliable ally in the sales process, someone who projects both confidence and competence. If you come across as anything less than capable and trustworthy, women customers will pick it up. For this reason, it's important to be fully aware of the verbal and nonverbal messages you send.

WHAT THIS MEANS FOR YOU

When everything about you conveys a sense of confidence that is genuine and compelling, women customers react by placing their trust in you.

HOW TO BRIDGE THE D-GENE

The biggest challenge for sale professionals—for everyone, really—is to *feel* confident so you can *project* confidence. On the other hand, you can feel confident and still send out messages women will interpret differently—especially when they first meet you.

> ➤ *Develop a deep reservoir of product knowledge.* Increased product knowledge breeds self-confidence. If you get into situations where you feel as if you're winging it, go back and do some more homework. Remember, the point is not to overwhelm your customer with product details, but to develop enough product knowledge to feel confident you can handle any situation. Your confidence is what she's looking for.

> ➤ *Smile.* A smile is one of a salesperson's greatest under-used tools. There's no more powerful way to let your customers know you're at ease and feeling good about what you're doing.

> ➤ *Behave confidently.* Did you know that research shows that if you behave confidently, you'll come to feel more confident? (This is known in some circles as the "fake it 'til you make it" rule.) Your mother had it right: stand up straight. Don't slouch. Develop a firm (as versus bone-crushing) handshake. Look the other person in the eye. Don't mumble. Speak clearly with an upbeat tone in your voice.

You need to bring these principles into play in all the work you do with your women customers. But there is one time when they absolutely have to be front and center, and that's during what we call the Two-Minute Take-Off.

5 THE TWO-MINUTE TAKEOFF

Hitting on All Five Principles

Let's take a moment to review where we are. You learned about just how big the women's market is for banking and brokerage services. You learned about the D-gene: how men and women are different, and why it matters to your success. We talked about five principles you can follow that will help you demonstrate your trustworthiness, which is the first thing women look for in a salesperson—as in, if she doesn't trust you, you're toast.

OK. You've absorbed all that, in a cerebral sort of way, and are about to have a conversation with a customer of the feminine persuasion. You've spoken briefly on the phone. Now she's at your office door. What do you do?

Maybe you should wing it. After all, you no doubt already have experience working with customers—maybe a lot—and no one's ever run screaming from your office. However, what if someone told you that within the first two minutes of meeting you, a woman will decide whether or not you are someone she can do business with?

And here's something else to think about: when a woman meets you for the first time, she may already have some half-conscious preconceptions about you, based on her prior experiences with other salespeople. You know what they are, right? The concern that you won't take her seriously. That you'll take

49

advantage of her relative lack of financial experience. And if you're a man, that you might even make a pass.

Not fair, you say? You're right, it isn't, but that's the way life is sometimes.

Your first task is not to take this personally. These preconceptions are not about you—specifically. You may be the most D-gene-savvy person on the planet, but you are still a salesperson, and as such you come with a certain amount of baggage. And we'll say it clearly, if you are a male salesperson, you probably come with a bigger load of baggage.

Does this mean she's a raging feminist? Absolutely not. Does she have a chip on her shoulder? Not at all. Let's just say that she's got very good reasons to be alert to any signs that she's not being taken seriously.

If you are a female salesperson, does any of this apply? Not in any gender-related way, of course, but the underlying anxiety and distrust may still be there. Read on to find out more.

Obviously you'll want to make sure you are observing each of the five principles of trust-based selling in your first meeting, because you'll never get a second chance to make a first impression, as the saying goes. So, we've put together the *Maddox Smye Never-Fail Steps to a Successful Two-Minute Takeoff*. Very short and sweet. Ready?

Step 1. Go to her. Don't make her come to you.

Why? Think back to when you were in high school and you had to walk across the gym floor to ask a girl or a guy to dance. How did you feel? Exposed? Vulnerable? Unsure of yourself? She's feeling a little like that now. It's up to you to create a safe environment in which she can open up and start sharing the reason for her visit. The safer and more comfortable she feels, the easier it will be for you to create the kind of relationship she's looking for—one that will result in increased sales.

So if you see her in your waiting room, walk out to greet her. If she appears in your office doorway, come around your desk and walk to her.

Step 2. Shake her hand.

Women are touchier—in the sense of liking to touch—than men. On the other hand, any touching between the sexes in the workplace these days is generally a bad idea, especially if it's initiated by a man—except for the handshake. So take the initiative. Don't wait for her to offer her hand; in the business world we've gone beyond that bit of Victorian etiquette. This is all about extending yourself, so extend your hand and shake her hand firmly. If you're a man, shake her hand in much the way you would shake a man's hand, remembering, of course, that your hand is probably bigger than hers and your grip may be stronger.

Step 3. Introduce yourself—slowly.

You probably already know that whenever people approach a discussion of their finances, their anxiety level goes up—sometimes way up. Anxious people can't listen very well. As a money manager once told us, "When it comes to talking about clients' money, I've gotten used to saying everything three times."

So take your time when you tell her your name, especially if it's a mouthful. Give her a card so she can read it. Names are often easier to understand when people can see them.

Step 4. Maintain eye contact and SMILE.

Women make and maintain eye contact more than men. That's part of the D-gene, as you learned in Chapter 3. Watch a man who is introduced to someone, male or female. Very shortly after meeting, his eyes will begin to shift—to other people in the room, to a picture on the wall, to his shoes, to nothing much at all. To a woman, this behavior literally looks shifty, and makes her wonder what he's really thinking. (We assume we don't need to explain a woman's reaction to a man who does his eye-shifting up and down her body.)

If you find it hard to sustain eye contact, do what actors do: focus on one eye, or pick a spot between the other person's eyes and concentrate on that.

Don't forget to smile. When you smile upon first meeting a customer, you're conveying a lot: I'm happy to meet you, I like what I'm doing, I feel confident that I can help you and that we will work well together. You probably can't fake a smile—not one you'd want anybody to see—but you can encourage the kinds of positive, upbeat feelings that will make you feel like smiling. So make the effort to put yourself in a positive mood: a genuine smile is hard to resist.

Step 5. Offer refreshments.

Research shows that the more senses you can engage, the stronger the connection you can create. What creates a stronger connection than sharing food or a beverage? Stale office coffee doesn't count.

With one hand tied behind your back, you can do better than that. How about special blends? A selection of teas? Soft drinks? Cookies? Candies? Some halfway decent cups and saucers? You are the host, after all, welcoming a guest to your office. Get things set up now, and you'll be ready when she arrives.

One more hint: if you can serve the refreshments yourself—instead of calling on a female assistant—you'll be way ahead of the game. Sad to say, women are seldom served by men. When they are, it makes a big impression.

That's it. Five simple steps to a two-minute takeoff. We told you it wouldn't take long.

Now you're ready to move into the sales conversation itself.

6 MASTERING THE ART OF FEMALE-FOCUSED LISTENING

How to Uncover Her Unique Needs and Wants

"You're not listening!"

If the average man pocketed a nickel for each time he got this complaint from a woman, his pants would fall down.

Let's face it, guys. You are notorious for not listening to women, even women customers. You know you're supposed to—they're customers, after all—but still you find yourself tuning out. Why? If you're honest with yourself, you'll probably admit to one or more of these reasons:

> ➤ I know in 45 seconds what she needs.

> ➤ I've heard it all before.

> ➤ I've heard it all before *from her.*

> ➤ I know what she means.

> ➤ I know what she's trying to say.

> ➤ Most of what she's saying is irrelevant.

No wonder one of the first questions men ask in our workshops is not, "How can I learn to listen better?" but "How can I get her to shut up?"

These men don't like our answer—which is "you can't"—until they realize how they can turn this initial part of the sales process into the beginning of a profitable buying and selling partnership.

So, let's assume you've successfully achieved a Two-Minute Takeoff with a woman customer. What's your next move? (Pick one of the following.)

A. Lock in her initial interest by making sure she knows your stellar qualities as a salesman who is D-gene-certified.

B. Ask her what she's looking for.

C. Ask how you can help her make the best use of her time.

You probably said "C," because you figured the correct answer to multiple-choice questions like these is usually the third choice. You're right, but do you know *why?*

The answer goes back to the second principle of trust-based selling: Respect her, her time, and her timing. By asking her how you can make the best use of her time, you're showing respect for the fact that she probably has every minute of her day accounted for and you want to make sure you don't take too much of her time.

"HELP" OR "HELPFUL"?

Do you know why "How can I be most helpful to you today?" is a better question than "How can I help you today?"

Because the first question focuses on how you can serve her, while the second implies that she's weak and needs help.

Small point? Maybe, but small points add up.

The interview process that's typically used with first-time customers of financial services is male-oriented. By that, we mean it is built around the concept of screening, of eliminating "extraneous" information, of quickly zeroing in on the "main points," the "key facts," the "action items." This process reveals men's preference for arriving at a narrow focus, and organizing information around that focus.

The box on the next page shows the type and order of information on a typical financial analysis form. Even though we left out all the blank lines for the information, you can see

Client Name: Date:

Personal Information: age, date of birth, children etc.

Employer: how long employed, annual income, life and health insurance provided, retirement programs.

Other types of insurance: company, face amount, premium, expiration date

Assets and liabilities

ASSETS	**LIABILITIES**
Savings	Rent
Checking	Auto Loan
IRAs	Credit Cards
Mutual Funds	Other Loans
Stock	Mortgage

Goals/Concerns:

1. _____   2. _____

3. _____   4. _____

5. _____   6. _____

Cash needs analysis

_____

_____

_____

Notes

_____

_____

_____

_____

WHAT SHE'S LOOKING FOR

Are you "merely" doing a good job, or do you really care about what she's telling you?

how tempting it is to simply take the customer through the items and write down what he or she says.

This is not the preferred process for most women, even though they may have no trouble going along with it. If left to their own devices, however, many women would start with the notes section. (Once they start talking, this is probably what they'll do anyway, so you might as well relax and enjoy the ride.)

If a man likes to focus, a woman likes to share. To make a good decision, she wants to know the whole picture, and as her broker or banker, she thinks you should, too. So when you take her through your series of screening questions, she's perfectly capable of answering them, but they make her a little anxious: Are you really listening to her? Are you "getting" her situation? Do you understand the dynamics of her life enough to make the kinds of recommendations that will suit her best?

In other words, women don't want to answer yes-or-no questions. They want you to understand their lives—not because they think they're so fascinating, but because this is the kind of information they'd want if they were in your position.

That's at the level of information. At another level, sharing information is part of a woman's way of building a relationship. She's telling you about her family, or her work, or her goals and concerns as a way of establishing common ground. As one broker with a lot of women clients put it, "When you work with a woman, you establish a relationship not just with her but with everything in her life that she takes care of, or worries about, or feels responsible for."

SLOW DOWN

You're not barreling down the Interstate. You're touring the local roads— and learning a great deal about your customer as you go.

Meanwhile, of course, your clock is ticking. You have appointments. You have sales goals. The day is going by. As she talks, you may find yourself getting antsy and your attention wandering: How long is this going to take? What does she want from me? I wonder if the Lakers won.

Fair enough: you've got your agenda, and she's got hers. The only thing is: she is the customer. Here's what we're saying: if you can find a way to tune in to her—*her* way—you'll be well rewarded.

In this chapter, we're going to tell you four things you can do to uncover her unique needs and wants in a female-focused way. Before we get started, however, you need to let go of any previous plans or preconceptions you may have had about the meeting's outcome. Think of what you're doing in this conversation as beginning a process, not working toward a specific outcome. Taking the time to get to know her and her expectations will help establish your credibility. It shows her you value her and the relationship as much as you do a sale—and gives her the confidence of knowing your recommendations will be uniquely suited to her special needs and circumstances.

1. TAP INTO HER STORY

Most salespeople in financial services are trained by their companies to take prospective customers through a series of qualifying questions. In our seminars, people often ask us for a standard list of screening questions geared to women. "It doesn't have to be long," one young man said. "In fact, it's better if it's short, on one side of the page, so I can have it in my lap or top desk drawer to refer to."

Sorry, guys. There is no such screening list that's geared to women. It just doesn't fit the D-gene. Instead, you need to be prepared for a wide-ranging back-and-forth conversation, with lots of detours and digressions. It might not seem very organized, from a man's point of view, but if you commit to tracking with her you'll hear most of what you need for both your immediate and future use.

Here are some topics and brief excerpts from the conversation of a woman at her first meeting with a broker. (Note that she was referred to him by one of his other women customers. As we said: once a woman decides you're trustworthy, she'll tell everyone about you.)

> *Ann has told me how happy she is with you, so I thought we should talk. . . . My husband died two years ago. . . . I now have a broker . . . he's so busy, must be a sign that he's successful . . . my son, Ronnie, a marketing VP in a high-tech company . . . says I have the right to as many meetings as I need in order to feel comfortable about my investments. . . . He's been a tremendous help. I never want to be a burden to him. . . . My daughter loves dogs, all kinds of animals, really. Would you believe she keeps gerbils in her underwear drawer? . . . She's only 14, but she has her heart set on being a vet. . . . My husband had the financial brains in the family. . . . I'd like to do something . . . my friends say I could do catering, but that seems like so much work at my age . . . my daughter-in-law has a home decorating business she runs from her house. I don't know how she does it. . . .*

> *The questions you ask should not be intended to make you look smart. Their purpose is to get her talking about what she wants and needs.*

If you can forget for a moment about what she's not telling you—her assets, her liabilities, her budget, et cetera—and tune into what she *is* saying, you'll pick up a treasure trove of information you can use now and in the future to provide the kind of proactive service that will result in increased sales:

1. Suggest quarterly meetings with her to review her account. With her permission, invite her son to attend.

2. Offer to have statements sent to him as well as to her, again with her permission.

3. Give her your home or cell phone number, so she can always reach you.

4. Offer to discuss strategies that address her concerns of becoming a burden: long-term health care insurance, lifetime income annuities, guaranteed investments.

5. Tell her about your friend who has a catering business. With your friend's permission, suggest that your customer might want to get together to learn more about the business.

6. Ask if she'd like to hear about some tuition savings ideas.

7. Make a note to track stories and events that feature kids and animals, and successful home businesses (especially catering).

Before you start asking questions, there are a few key steps you need to take. First, explain that you're going to be seeking information about her situation that will help you make the best possible recommendations for her. Let her know that you'll be taking notes, and that she should feel free to interrupt at any time if she has a question.

> *In order to do the best job for you, I need to know what's important to you. So I'll be asking questions, and taking notes on what you say. If you have questions at any point in this process, please ask. That's part of my job.*

Ask how you can be most helpful to her at this meeting. Clarify how much time she has.

> *How can we make the best use of your time right now?*

Start with the broad, open-ended questions. Be sure to include questions that allow her to tell you about issues of importance in her life.

> *What would you say are your priorities and concerns?*

> *How do you see your situation now?*

> *What outcomes are you looking for?*

> *What expectations do you have of me and my organization?*

Unless she has already interviewed several other brokers, chances are she won't have sound-bite answers to any of these questions. Instead she'll do what most of us do—men as well as women—which is to use the process of answering to think through what she means, adding layers of context as she talks. You can strengthen your connection with her by creating a judgment-free zone in which she can think through her needs, asking for your advice when she needs it.

2. STAY TUNED INTO HER

Just paying attention is not enough. You need to show her that you're paying attention.

This is another one of those D-gene moments. Men and women behave differently when they're listening. Men may not make eye contact. They may look distracted, or out the window, or lost in thought. They may have a frown on their faces. None of this means they're not listening; quite the contrary, they may be concentrating deeply.

When women are listening, on the other hand, they don't just sit there. They make eye contact. They nod. They *respond*. They *react physically*. They share their own experiences in an effort to draw the other person closer. All this, to a woman, is listening. What a man does is . . . something else, she's not quite sure what. Since she's already anxious about not being taken seriously, it's easy for her to leap to conclusions when she sees you just sitting there. Maybe you're bored, she thinks. Maybe you think she's stupid. Maybe you're just waiting to contradict her.

Your challenge, therefore, is to pay attention *visibly*. Here's how:

Show her you're listening. Demonstrate your interest through eye contact, head nods, voice tone, and short phrases.

SHE: *Last Thursday night at 10:30 I was on my cell phone, waiting for my luggage at the Pittsburgh airport while my assistant read me a draft of a press release that had to go out the next day. That's crazy.*

YOU: *Ten-thirty⸘! I'm brain-dead at ten-thirty.*

SHE: *Me too! That's why I have to get off this merry-go-round.*

YOU: *Sounds like selling your business is a higher priority than it was at our first meeting.*

SHE: *You know . . . I think you're right.*

YOU: *Yeah. You sound ready.*

SHE: *I am! I am good and ready!*

Listen with your eyes as well as your ears. What message are her body language and facial expressions giving you⸘ Is it different from what she's saying⸘ You may want to comment on the discrepancy directly:

YOU: *I know you say you're excited about this investment, but you don't seem excited, somehow.*

Or you may want to tuck this information away, so that—for example—you have an alternative recommendation ready if she changes her mind.

3. ASK HER QUESTIONS TO CLARIFY MEANING, FEELINGS, AND DETAILS

Once she's answered your broad questions, you'll need to sift and sort through what she's told you in order to tailor a solution that's best for her. The more you can link your questions back to something specific she said, or an emotional state, the more she'll realize that you were really listening. Here are some clarifying questions you can ask:

You said you need to do something right away. What's your time frame?

What happened to make that experience so frustrating for you?

It sounds like you would prefer not to sell any securities at this time. Did I understand that correctly?

What sum of money would give you that sense of security you're looking for?

Make sure your questions reflect your need for clarification or for more information, rather than any suggestion that she's not expressing herself clearly. Since women tend to be self-deprecating, you may need to go out of your way not to give this impression.

Make it as easy as possible for her to provide information. Many people—men as well as women—resist any kind of financial planning. Some approach money the same way they approach getting in shape: they mean to, they know it's important, but somehow they always find an excuse for avoiding it. You may well get partial answers to your questions about assets, obligations, and goals. You may need to sit down with your customer and a shoebox full of records to help her sort things out.

Is it worth your time to hold a prospect's hand like this? It was for a midwestern broker with a customer whose mother needed help. The broker ended up spending a weekend afternoon in the mother's garage, going through two shopping bags of financial records and literally making piles of papers on the garage floor. The broker got some business from the mother, but the mother's other two children were so grateful for his help that they each shifted their sizeable accounts to him. "Both children have children of their own," he said. "I'm now the financial adviser for the whole family."

4. CONVEY YOUR UNDERSTANDING SO SHE KNOWS SHE'S BEEN HEARD

Women want to know they've been understood correctly. They want to make sure you got the facts, but they also want to know you understand the important nuances of their situation. So at key points in your discussion, play back your understanding of the facts and how she feels about them.

"You've worked hard on fixing up that rental property. It sounds like you'd rather not sell, if there's some other way to generate income, even if it's slightly less than you'd get from the proceeds of a sale."

You need to make sure your understanding is accurate, because it will become the basis of the subsequent work you do with her.

Don't be surprised if you don't get it right the first time. She may have given you a great deal of big-picture information to process, and it may take you some time to extract the meaning she intended. Don't let this bother you; this kind of collaborative process is embedded in the D-gene. Besides, there are benefits of not getting it right the first time:

> ➤ She gets to explain some more—which translates into more bonding.

> ➤ She gets to correct you—which if it doesn't happen too often, will make you seem more human to her. Besides, what woman doesn't like to correct a man?

By the same token, she may well change her mind when she hears your summary. Keep in mind it's not what she told you but the understanding both of you eventually arrive at that is important.

Pitfalls

> ➤ *Don't short-circuit the process by telling her what she wants.* You may be right; after all, this is your job, and you speak to customers every day. Even so, you're robbing the customer of the ability to crystallize her thoughts and share them with you. You're also neglecting the relationship-building that happens when she tells you her story.

> ➤ *Don't pepper her with questions.* You're not a trial lawyer, and she's not a hostile witness. Avoid a series of closed questions, especially those that call for a yes or no answer. After you ask a question, give her plenty of time to answer. Add your reactions to what she said before you jump in with the next question.

> ➤ *Avoid leading questions.* Women are especially sensitive to questions that seem to manipulate or patronize. "You want to save money, don't you?" or "I'm sure you'd agree that…" fall into this category.

> ➤ *Keep your distance.* Avoid a listening stance that leans into her personal space and makes her feel threatened.

> ➤ *Don't interrupt.* If you think we're repeating ourselves on this topic, it's because we are.

> ➤ *Create some moments of silence.* You don't want to just sit there till she says something; after all, you're not a psychoanalyst. Still, a few gentle silences will have the effect of encouraging her to open up, especially if you then respond with nods and phrases of understanding.

The Next Phase

If everything has been going well, you've reached a common understanding about what your customer wants. You've begun to feel more comfortable with each other. By showing your respect and interest in her as a person rather than just a customer, you're ready to move on to the next phase in the process, which is offering recommendations that you think will best meet her unique needs.

Don't be surprised if you don't move to this phase at the end of your first meeting, or even your second. It's part of the D-gene to be very thorough and to talk to other people about you to see what they think.

She'll let you know when she's ready. At this point, you need to move from a fairly free-wheeling conversation to a discussion of solutions: products, services, recommendations. Your challenge will be to make this shift without leaving behind the conversational, collaborative tone you have worked hard to establish.

TURNING YOUR PRESENTATION INTO A CONVERSATION

How to Share the Information She Wants, the Way She Wants It

One of the things we love most about good salespeople is their enthusiasm for the product or service they're selling. It's a pleasure to deal with people who are passionate about their work, and convinced that what they are selling is exactly what you need. Can you imagine making a major purchase from someone who lacks this quality?

Probably not. However, . . .

Early on in the selling process, your customers—and especially your women customers—aren't ready for any heavy-duty selling. Women appreciate your passion, but what they're really after at this point is information—and not just any information, either, but information that responds specifically to their concerns. Otherwise, they're likely to think they're being hustled. Of course, men don't like to be hustled either, but they are usually able to dismiss it as part of the selling game. Women, on the other hand, tend to take it personally: does this person really think I'm stupid enough to buy this line of bull? If they think they're being hustled, they're likely to leave and never come back.

What this means is, if you had planned to give a canned presentation to your woman customer, you might want to rethink your decision. Your challenge instead is to maintain the conversational approach that you adopted when you were asking her about her needs—and still give her the information and/or recommendations she needs to make a decision.

Canned Presentations? Who, Me?

The ability to shift seamlessly from asking about her needs to offering information or making recommendations about your product is the hallmark of trusted advisers. It's a natural shift for them because they don't have the "now it's time to sell her something" mind-set. They see the whole experience in terms of constantly refining their knowledge of the customer—first of her needs, and then of how best to match their products with those needs.

Even though you may not make what you think of as a canned presentation, as an experienced salesperson you probably have certain approaches and patterns of speech—phrases or even whole paragraphs—that you have found effective when talking with customers about your products and services. Since in all probability most of your customers have been men, you may want to reexamine some of these "sure-fire" lines and techniques in light of how effective they are with women.

Here's a quick quiz to help you conduct an inventory:

	YES	NO
1. I use a lot of sports and military analogies.		
2. I typically present information for three minutes or more without interruption.		

	YES	NO
3. I focus more on features than on benefits.		
4. I add value by making strong recommendations, since I'm more aware of the consequences of these decisions than most of my customers.		
5. Although I don't make canned presentations, I do rely on a few key slides to explain my product or service.		
6 To move customers along, I sometimes use phrases like "you'll never go wrong . . . ," "this opportunity won't last forever . . . ," and "you can trust me when I tell you . . . ."		
7. I use a lot of humor to make my points.		
8. I use phrases like "If you're like most people..."		
9. I describe benefits in terms of increased status, e.g., "this will help you really stand out from the crowd."		
10. I use a lot of directive terms—"you should," "you'll have to," and "you need to."		

None of these approaches is D-gene-friendly—with the possible exception of humor. We include it here because the particular humor that has proven effective with male customers might not necessarily work well with women.

People in our training seminars frequently ask us about pre-pared presentations aimed at women. If a standard version works with men, they want to know, why couldn't someone put together a presentation that was D-gene-friendly?

First of all, we question whether prepared presentations are as effective with men as many salespeople think. Leaving that aside, however, just as we've never seen a standard screening set of questions, we've never come across a scripted presentation that works terribly well with a woman customer. One reason is that a woman has too many questions that take the presenter too far afield for a single script to be much of a guide. A bigger reason, however, is that a woman is looking for a unique solution that responds specifically to what she told you; the slightest whiff of something canned will cause her to question just how much you really understand her needs.

So if you can't use your salesman shtick, what's left? Four skills that will enable you to give her the information she wants without undercutting your role as a trusted adviser.

1. MAKE IT A TWO-WAY STREET

Men, you'll remember, talk in longer chunks of time than women do. Women talk in shorter chunks, and they also take turns talking by pausing to give the other person a chance to step in. But realistically speaking, at this point you may have more to tell her than she has to tell you (although if you haven't done a good job of listening, this may not be true). So what do you do?

First, ask her what information she wants and the best way for you to provide it. The idea is to make sure she stays in charge of the process at all times. The following comparison illustrates the difference between telling her what she needs to know and putting her in the driver's seat.

GENERIC APPROACH	D-GENE-FRIENDLY APPROACH
It's a really solid company. I'd recommend it to anybody.	What would you like to know about this company?
Remind me before you leave to give you a packet of information.	Would you like a couple of articles to read? Or would you like me to set up a meeting with . . .
There are basically three things you need to know about this policy.	What features of this policy should we go over?

Of course, you'll still need to make sure that she gets all the information she needs to make an informed decision.

These are the issues I see. Would you agree? Which are most important from your perspective?

What we're talking about here is a matter of emphasis: start with what *she* wants to know, instead of what *you* think she needs to know.

Answer her questions when she asks them, not when you would like to answer them. If you're one of those methodical people who eat all your peas and then all your mashed potatoes, even the thought of following this guideline could drive you crazy. All we're saying is, the more you can do to get on your customer's wavelength, the greater your chances of increasing your immediate sale—and the potential for additional sales down the road. It's your choice.

> **WHAT'S YOUR MENTAL IMAGE?**
>
> *Instead of thinking of a presentation as giving a speech, imagine that you are an expert witness in a trial, being questioned by a friendly lawyer.*

Give brief, concise answers to her questions, and then ask her what else she'd like to know. You're the product expert, and it's tempting to take her question and run with it. Keep in mind, however, that while you may be the product

> **HOW TO PATRONIZE AND DISCOUNT A CUSTOMER**
>
> *"What a great question! I'll get to it in just a minute."*

expert, you're not the expert at knowing what she wants. As a general rule, you probably shouldn't talk for more than a minute or two without giving her an opportunity to respond.

Check in with her periodically to see if she's getting what she wants. You're not looking for a grade on your performance. You know she's on a tight schedule, and you want to make sure she's getting the information she needs to make a decision.

It's important to determine how she prefers to learn. Is it by reading? Listening? Seeing a visual? Many people—including many women—respond well to stories of people like themselves and how the product you're selling has solved a problem for them or improved their lives.

Until you know what kind of learner she is, try different approaches. Watch her face and see if she responds. If she seems uninterested in a factual explanation, you might say, "Here's another way to look at it," and put the information in story form.

2. TAKE WHAT YOU'VE LEARNED FROM HER AND USE IT

There's nothing more effective than linking back everything you say about your product or service to something she told you. It's a good selling practice in general, but it's especially effective when used with women.

This is another place where all the careful listening you did will pay off, by enabling you to make close links between what your product can do and what she has told you she wants:

This investment will pay enough to cover the mortgage on that cabin in the woods you were telling me about.

I took this approach because I know your work doesn't leave you much time to keep track of these things.

I thought you might want to consider this alternative-energy stock because of your son's interest in this field.

Here are some things you can do to let her know you're basing your suggestions and recommendations on what she told you:

> ➤ Refer to the notes you took.
> ➤ Use her exact words or phrases whenever possible. It's a good way to demonstrate your respect.
> ➤ Underscore any outcomes she feels strongly about.
>   *This will increase your post-retirement income, which I know is important to you.*
> ➤ If you're offering a range of suggestions, prioritize them based on what you've learned is important to her.

Since I know you want to stay away from technology stocks ...

> Use technical terms that match her level of knowledge and understanding.

> Select visual support, sales and marketing materials she'll find relevant and useful to share with others.

> Paint word pictures that help make your point.

I'm aware of your not wanting to get bogged down in details. I want our meetings to make you feel like you're getting a high-level view, as if you were looking down at the market from a hot-air balloon.

> Be enthusiastic about the solution you're recommending.

Of course, it goes without saying that customers also convey information about what they need less directly. If you've been tuning into her body language and tone of voice as well as her words, you may have picked up some unspoken concerns or fears. It's probably more effective to acknowledge these indirectly:

Many people are concerned about their ability to make the right decisions at the right time. The suggestions we're talking about today will free you up from that worry.

3. POSITION THE TOTAL CUSTOMER EXPERIENCE TO HER

Few if any of the products you sell are unique to you or your organization. If you want to distinguish yourself from your competition, you need to demonstrate other ways you can add value. One of the strongest differentiators, especially for women, is the post-sale service you and members of your team

---

THE 12-YEAR-OLD TEST

One broker said when she needed to explain a new investment instrument, she practiced on her 12-year-old daughter. "If she can understand, chances are good most of my customers will understand as well."

provide to make the experience as easy for her as you can. Make sure you relate the services provided to any unique needs of hers, keeping in mind that her greatest need is probably for more time.

A lot of people today don't have time to make sure their financial records are always in order. If you want to bring in what you have, we'll be happy to help you sort it out. Or would it be more convenient if I came to your house?

Here's my cell phone number. You can always reach me on it.

Assuming we move forward, you'll be getting a lot of paperwork associated with what we've been planning today. If you like, you can bring it in here and we can sort it out for you.

4. MAKE YOUR NETWORK HER NETWORK

One of your greatest assets is your roster of other satisfied customers. Consider them your fan club, and don't be afraid to call on them. If a woman customer has some concerns or objections, tell stories about satisfied customers who had similar concerns at first. Offer to put her in contact with customers who would be willing to share their experiences. Giving her the chance to share her situation and learn from others is a very D-gene-friendly way to resolve concerns. It removes you from the expert role, and enables her to get a sense of the kind of person you are from other customers.

Pitfalls

Here are some behaviors to avoid when you're sharing information about your product or service:

> *Bad-mouthing the competition.* It's not a good idea under any circumstances, but women find it especially objec-

tionable. How can they be sure that you won't bad-mouth them behind their backs?

> *Bragging.* Women are very suspicious of overt bragging. But don't worry. If you make sure your plaques, certificates, and awards are prominently displayed in your office, these inanimate objects will do your bragging for you.

> *"Talking down."* The trick here is to examine your assumptions. If you assume that women "can't understand figures" or "don't get technology," you need to update your thinking. Everyone learns and understands differently; one way is not better or worse than any other. (We won't bore you with the women who have made fortunes understanding figures and "getting" technology.) Keep in mind that the more you can adapt to your customers' preferences, the greater your chances of increasing your sales.

> *Lecturing.* Don't use her question or comment to launch into a lecture. Keep it conversational. Remember, her head-nodding means that she hears you, not that she agrees with you. If she does too much nodding, you're doing too much talking.

> *Humor.* Guys banter and rib each other as a way to make contact. Many women don't like it, so don't do it.

8 MAKING THE SALE HER WAY

How to Complete a Pressure-less Close

Let's be frank. No matter how much effort you put into creating a trust-based relationship with a customer, the fact remains that as a sales professional you make your living closing deals. Absolutely nothing wrong with that. Our whole purpose is to help you close more deals. The only problem is that the classic closing techniques, which are based primarily on manipulation ("What color should we order that in?"), don't work very well with women.

When it comes to closing, most salespeople know that customers don't like a hard sell, and they try not to appear too aggressive. If the customer is a woman, they may make an extra effort. Yet when they reach the point of wanting to close and the woman isn't ready—or doesn't *seem* ready—their good intentions can fly out the window, and they're suddenly all over her like threads on a cheap suit. The result: what had looked like a sure thing suddenly turns very, very cold.

Closing a deal can be a stressful experience. You've invested time in the customer, and you want it—you need it—to pay off.

> ### WHEN A WOMAN LEAVES...
>
> *When women meet with a salesperson, they always go in with an exit strategy—I've got to pick up my son from soccer practice, or I'm meeting a friend in 30 minutes. That way, if the meeting doesn't go well, they can leave without a confrontation or hurt feelings. The problem for the salesperson is that he may have lost a customer without ever knowing why.*

The greater your need, the greater the temptation to shift your focus from serving the customer to making the sale, even though you may know better. During periods of stress it's not unusual to fall back on old behaviors, even if you've come to believe they're not effective, simply because they're familiar. That's why, in your focus on closing, you might forget everything you've learned about the D-gene and default to high-pressure mode—which doesn't have to be very high to turn women off.

He Said, She Said

That's what happened to Victor, a financial adviser who had been working with a woman to prepare an investment plan that would permit her to retire in about 15 years. Things were going well until the day he went for the close. Here are his and hers versions of what happened:

HIS VERSION

It was the third meeting when it all went off the tracks. At the first meeting Mrs. Sterling came in with some documents. We talked about what she needed, and the meeting ended with both of us having some homework to do. At the second meeting I had put together a plan for her to consider. She had quite a few questions, but in general she seemed pleased.

She wanted to talk things over with her son-in-law, so we scheduled a third meeting. My understanding was we would set up an account for her then, and arrange for her funds and accounts to be transferred here, so I could start building the kind of portfolio we had been talking about for her.

This third meeting took place the last week of the month. Frankly, I hadn't had a very good month, so I was looking forward to getting her on the books. Her son-in-law liked the plan; I thought his approval was the final piece of the puzzle. I could tell she was ready to finalize the deal. She had a lot of questions, but she seemed to agree with all the answers I gave her.

When I showed her the papers she had to sign, which I had drawn up before she arrived, she nodded in agreement, but eventually she said she wanted to talk to a few more people. Apparently her chiropractor had been very successful in the market, and she wanted to bounce our plan off him.

Her chiropractor!¿ I didn't say anything, but it really made me mad that she would equate a chiropractor with a trained financial adviser. Anyway, I didn't want to spend any more time with her if she wasn't serious, so I started asking her some questions to find out where she stood. I figured if she didn't sign something before she left my office, I'd lose her. Right away she starts backing off and saying she needs more time, and she's running late, and 'don't call me, I'll call you.'

So that's that. I guess she was just shopping around.

HER VERSION

Too bad about Victor. I thought I'd finally found someone who understood me, until the day he got really pushy and obnoxious.

What Went Wrong?

In this part of the selling process it's very easy for a salesperson who doesn't understand the D-gene to misread or ignore a woman's signals, and as a result end up losing the sale.

In this case, the salesman's gut instinct that she was ready to buy was probably based on his experience with male customers. Also, as you now know, all her nodding meant only that she understood what he was saying, not that she agreed with it. Finally, when she said she wanted to think about it and talk to her chiropractor, she was not sending a "no interest" message.

Research into the D-gene indicates that, unlike men, when women say they want to do some more thinking and talk with other people, that's exactly what they mean.

It's part of a woman's collaborative nature to draw others into the process of helping her make decisions. It's also true that while men want to make a good decision, for a woman it has to be a *perfect* decision—one that meets all the many needs on a woman's radar screen, including the needs of all the people in her life. This need may also go back to the feeling that when it comes to finance, she's on foreign territory, and can't risk making a wrong move.

Meanwhile, the salesman, at the end of a "bad month," was caught up in his own perfectly understandable need to boost his sales. Unfortunately, the harder he tried, the worse the situation became.

One of the biggest lessons here is the importance of maintaining a balanced attitude.

> **BECAUSE MORE OF TODAY'S BUYERS ARE WOMEN?**
>
> The manager of a car dealership we work with said the percentage of customers they sell on the first visit has fallen from 21% to just over 14%.

Accept the fact that women are probably going to take longer to make a decision than your male customers. Don't think that if they leave your office without agreeing to buy you will have lost them. In most cases, they will come back. If you try to force them into a decision, on the other hand, they probably won't.

You need to approach the close in the belief that it is another step in the process of developing a relationship, and not the final step, either. Instead of worrying that you will lose the sale if you don't close now, adopt an attitude of abundance: you will sell your customer eventually—if not today, then tomorrow.

In addition to these "attitude adjustments," there are five specific steps you can take to keep your customer in charge of the selling process so that you can make the sale her way.

1. DRIVE THE PROCESS, NOT HER DECISION

Although you cannot shorten a woman's buying cycle to meet your needs, you can guide it: not pressuring her doesn't mean you should do nothing. While she wants to make the decision on her timetable, she also wants you to ease the process for her. Again, remember that for her this not a transaction; it's a *relationship* with a trusted adviser.

Let her set the pace by asking what she needs to move forward. Maybe it's more information. Maybe it's a review of information you've already provided.

What additional information can I get for you?

What's the best way to get it to you?

Act as her intermediary with other people or departments so she gets what she needs. Most of the time this is pretty straightforward: for example, collecting more data or helping with forms. Other help you could offer that might make more of an impression:

> ➤ Contact a lender and get a payoff balance for her.

> ➤ Call her company's human resources department to get information on the company's retirement plan options.

> ➤ Analyze the holdings of a fund to identify any that might constitute a conflict of interest for the customer.

2. HELP HER WEIGH EACH OPTION

Deciding where to put your money entails risk, so it's no wonder that a customer might want to go slow. If she's got a lot to consider, she'll appreciate your help in comparing the various options. One approach that keeps you out of the "pushing" mode is to go back to the priorities she gave you, and show her how the options measure up.

I recommended mutual funds because you told me you didn't want to get involved in making daily decisions about your investments. Do you still feel that way?

Ask her to describe the risks she sees. Don't try to talk her out of them.

When you think of putting your money in these investments, what risks come up for you?

What contingencies would you want in place to feel more secure?

Walk through the potential gains, downsides, and trade-offs of each option. Then compare the options with regard to their pluses and minuses.

Offer your best advice—when she asks for it. You may have to bite your tongue to keep from telling her what you think she should do. Try to remember that in helping her to come to her own conclusion, you're also continuing to build a relationship with her that could result in substantial future sales.

Demonstrate optimism, enthusiasm, and patience. Reaffirm that she's making an important decision and is right to be taking her time. Assure her that the approach she's taking will produce a decision she'll be happy with. Offer her your continuing support.

3. GIVE HER SOME ROOM

Many women will want some mental breathing space to think, talk with family and friends, and let everything sink in. Give her as much space as she needs. You might want to create a quiet spot in your office for her to review what she's learned. Offer her the use of a conference room to read and think. Make a phone available.

At the same time, make yourself available, and make sure she has several options for getting in touch with you.

The biggest challenge in waiting for her final decision may be managing your own anxiety. Having invested a lot of your time and energy, it's hard not knowing when—or if—the deal will go through. One way to reduce your uncertainty is to have already planned what your next move with her will be. Will you follow up with some more information? Suggest someone she could talk to?

Suggest a concrete plan for following up. The challenge here is to structure times to talk without crowding her.

Let's put a time on the calendar to get together and see where we are, maybe early next week. What day works for you?

What's the best way to follow up with you?

Support her desire to involve others in her decision-making. Don't take it personally; it doesn't mean that she doesn't trust or respect your opinion.

Would you like duplicate copies of these articles to share with others?

I'd be happy to talk with your daughter, if you'd like me to.

4. HELP HER FINALIZE HER DECISION

Because a woman will notice if you start to shift your focus from her to closing the sale, make sure you stress the importance to you of the relationship by looking back with her over what you've done to arrive at this point. Offer plenty of affirmations that she has made the right decision. Make it clear that you have enjoyed working with her and look forward to working together in the future.

Recap the outcomes she's looking for, and how her decision will provide them.

By the time Robin's ready for college, you should have a substantial nest egg for her tuition.

Nail down any loose ends; she'll appreciate your attention to detail. Incidentally, make sure you find a graceful way to let her know what you've done for her. First, your efforts on her behalf will further cement your relationship. She should know about them, if you can let her know without appearing to brag. Also, if she's not financially savvy, she will probably appreciate learning the ins and outs of these transactions.

Express your endorsement of her decision. Many buyers have moments of insecurity and doubt after making a major purchase; this is especially true for women in traditionally male industries. Also, at some level the better she feels about her decision, the better she will feel about you as the person who helped her reach it.

"I gave you a lot of information to sift through, and I think you've made an excellent decision."

5. DON'T ALLOW A "NO" TO END THE PROCESS

If she decides not to move ahead, keep the relationship open. Act as if it will continue. Don't automatically assume that you did something wrong, or that she is not interested in what you are selling. Women lead complicated lives, and there may well have been outside factors that caused her to say no.

A luxury car salesman we heard about ruined a sale by getting suspicious when a woman he had been working with appeared to back out of a sale. She was getting a healthy bonus from her company, and was planning to use it to buy herself a car. They'd worked out a price for the car and the features she wanted. She told him she would sign the papers on Friday, when she expected her bonus check to come through.

Her check didn't arrive on Friday, so she called the salesperson to say she'd have to wait until it did. Thinking this was a bargaining ploy on her part, he started applying pressure to buy now—giving her $500 off the price, throwing in leather seats. "It made me angry that he didn't take my word," she said. "I thought we had a pretty good relationship and suddenly he's hustling me. Also, I started wondering just how firm the price was. I ended up going elsewhere."

So keep the door open. She may be feeling guilty for taking so much of your time and then not buying. Alleviate her concerns by sharing your enthusiasm for working with her in the future.

I'm sorry this didn't work out, but I enjoyed working with you and hope we can work together in the future.

Create excuses to reach out. This is where your female-focused listening can pay off. If you share a common interest, use it to stay in touch. If she said she liked a certain author, and you read a review of his latest book, send it to her with a brief note.

Some salespeople make a point of having an additional piece of nonessential information they can use as a reason for a follow-up call.

Assume that you will work together in the future, and act accordingly. Invite her to seminars you present. Update her on the financial instruments you discussed. Include her in occasional mailings you send out (preferably from you, rather than from your company).

Finally, ask for her feedback on how you might have better met her needs.

I'd really appreciate your feedback on what I might have done differently.

Take in what she says, and use it with your other women customers. A customer's honest feedback is a real gift. She's under no obligation to take the time to tell you what she thinks of your performance, so listen with an open mind everything she tells you. Don't get defensive, or try to convince her of what you were trying to do. Just take it all in, and when she's done, express your gratitude for her insights.

Pitfalls

Closing is a high-stakes moment. Any one of several pitfalls can be enough to spoil the deal.

> ➤ *Assuming she's not the decision-maker.* There's no quicker way to ruin a sale than by hinting that she might not be the decision-maker. So assume she is, until and unless she tells you otherwise.

> ➤ *Misreading her nods.* In earlier chapters we talked about the fact that men nod to express agreement, women to express understanding. As you approach the close, however, you might revert to your default understanding. So be careful: just because you want her to agree, don't assume she does.

> ➤ *Rushing her.* Anything you do to hurry her along takes away her control of the situation. It also undercuts the impression that you're focused more on the relationship than on the outcome.

> ➤ *Poor-mouthing.* Don't attempt to win her sympathy by hinting at how much you need this sale. It's a manipulation; she won't like it, or respect you for using it.

To sum up: if you can maintain a positive attitude, focus on what the customer wants and on nurturing the relationship, you can complete a pressure-less close. One of the outcomes is a mutual understanding that, in terms of the relationship, it isn't a close at all, but just another step in the buying and selling process.

9 SUPPORTING HER THROUGH THE SALE

How to Provide Seamless, Nonintrusive Administration

Now that she's decided to buy, is she history? Is your mind is racing ahead to your next sale? Are you looking for the earliest possible moment when you can hand her over to your assistant, or to whatever part of your company provides after-sale support?

We hope not.

We know there are companies that encourage their salespeople to pass a customer along as soon as possible so they can get back out into the fray and sell, sell, sell. Chances are these companies have never heard of the D-gene.

Once you understand the perspective of a woman customer who has reached this point in her buying process, you'll understand why it's so critical to provide her with continuing support.

For your customer, the decision to buy represents the beginning of a longer-term relationship with you, not the end. At some level she sees everything that has led up to this point almost as a kind of courtship. Her decision to buy is a reward not only for the quality of your recommendations, but also for your attentive listening, and your willingness to "do it her way." She likes your enthusiasm, and your understanding of the uniqueness of her situation. In

> **"I DO"**
>
> *When a woman makes the decision to buy, in her mind it's a little like moving from dating to marriage.*

short, because you seem to be someone she can trust and work with successfully over the long haul, she has cast her lot with you.

Living in Limbo

This period of time between the decision to buy and the final execution of the sale is a kind of limbo—for salespeople and customers alike. Salespeople, having achieved their objective, tend to put less energy into the relationship. From here on in, they would like to think, it's all paperwork. Customers, having decided to buy, are often surprised and sometimes confused by all the additional steps and decisions required to finalize the deal.

Your understanding of the D-gene presents you with an unequaled opportunity to provide the kind of service during this part of the selling process that will set you apart from your competition, and build her confidence that the decision she made is the right one. Given that most of the products you sell are available elsewhere, this is where you begin to add real value in the form of the peace of mind you create for her.

> **BECAUSE SHE CAN STILL CHANGE HER MIND**
>
> *After she decides to buy, there are more decisions to make. During this time she needs to know she can continue to rely on you. If you take your eye off the ball, you could lose yourself a customer.*

In other words, this is no time to let down and relax. Given everything you've done for her so far, you can be sure she will have great expectations of your continuing high level of commitment during this next phase of the sale. She's going to be very alert to any indication that your interest in her has cooled, or that your primary focus is the sale, and not the relationship.

You need to be as energetic and committed as you were before. This means finding ways to make all transactions as simple and convenient as possible for her. Your efforts will build trust and loyalty in the short term and positive word of mouth in the long term.

1. BE HER AMBASSADOR

Even though her primary relationship is with you, in order to execute the sale she will probably still need to work with others in your organization. To see that she's well treated, and to protect your relationship with her, it's in your best interest to make sure these transactions go smoothly, and to step in when they don't.

If it's possible, intercede on her behalf. Can you complete a form for her that's required by another department? Does she need to submit documents to another department? Could you do it for her?

Remember how busy she is likely to be. Are there procedures you could streamline for her? Penalties you could waive? Deadlines you could circumvent? She'll appreciate your efforts to remove roadblocks and smooth the way.

> **MAKE FRIENDS WITH YOUR BACK OFFICE**
>
> *The people you rely on to expedite a customer transaction are often overworked and under-appreciated. If you made it a point to recognize their efforts and find ways to let them know how important they are, do you think they would give your customers special attention?*
>
> *We bet they would.*

This approach is in direct opposition to the "if I did it for you, I'd have to do it for everybody" treatment. In fact, special treatment is exactly what women want. (It's what everybody wants, although it has a bigger positive impact on women because of what it says about the relationship.) It's up to you to figure out how to provide it without breaking the law or getting fired. In other words, this is where your creativity comes into play.

Here's an example of creativity in action:

> **YOUR CHALLENGE**
>
> *The idea is to make things as easy as possible for her—without breaking the law or getting fired.*

A woman we know had decided to switch all her considerable assets—investments, checking accounts, mortgages, credit cards, lines of credit—to a large financial services company. She had been impressed with the people she had met at this firm; the service they promised seemed appropriate for a customer of her considerable and complex set of assets.

However, as she and the new company were going through the lengthy process of closing and opening accounts and transferring funds, she ran into a problem. There was a house she wanted to buy, tear down, and replace with one of her own design. She needed the company to put together a complex credit package that would save her some interest by leveraging her existing assets.

"The people in their mortgage division told me that what I was asking for was against their policy," she remembers. "I liked that they felt a responsibility to follow their policy, but I'm also thinking, 'Hmm, the broker I'd talked to had said he would work with me closely to see I got whatever I needed.' Maybe I'd made a mistake.

"It was Friday afternoon. About four o'clock the broker called up and said he'd just heard what happened, and that if I gave him until Monday noon, he'd work something out. I couldn't do anything until Monday anyway. So—long story short, he called Monday to say he hadn't gotten anywhere with people in his own mortgage department, so he'd gone to another lender and convinced him to put together the package I wanted. He said he'd take care of everything. As far as I was concerned, it would be as if I was working with his company.

"It was extraordinary, what he did," she said, "And it gave me a great story to tell."

Being her ambassador probably won't always involve such extreme measures. There are, however, other ambassadorial steps you can take.

You can introduce her to your business partners. Explain what they do and state your confidence in their abilities and willingness to help. Show her that you respect each other and work well together as a team. She'll appreciate that. (And by business partners, we mean office as well as professional staff. Show them the same respect you show to your professional colleagues. You'll earn points with your customer. Besides, it's the right thing to do.)

If your company requires you to hand off your customer, you can still have a hand-off plan of your own. Assuming diminishing personal contact, there are still ways you can help. At first, for example, you may be able to call the people she needs to work with yourself. Later, you might want to provide her with a list of names and extensions, and check in with her from time to time to make sure she's reaching the right people.

Explain your customer's situation to others in your organization who might be working with her. It will keep her from having to explain herself over and over. If you include some appropriate personal aspect of her story, it will help your colleague put a face on someone who would otherwise be just a name on a list. For example, instead of simply directing the back office to send a duplicate statement to her son, you might add that he is the VP of finance for a high-tech company, and that she values his input.

In addition to handling matters for her personally, here are two other actions that will let her know she is very much on your radar screen:

> ➤ Ask her how she would like you to contact her in the future—by phone, fax, or email—and how often. Or would she prefer always to call you? Would she like regular contact, or only as needed? It's a good idea to let her know the preferences of some of your other customers, so she knows what she can ask for.

> ➤ In a letter to her, describe the kind of assistance you can best provide, and the kind of help your assistant is best equipped to offer.

2. DELIVER COMFORT, NOT STRESS

Because most women are care-givers for other people, they'll be especially appreciative of your efforts to take care of them. Anything you can do to lighten their load will make a big difference to them—in terms of time and effort saved, and the psychological security that comes from knowing someone is looking out for you.

Some salespeople tend to stress the problems and difficulties involved, in order to make their efforts to help seem more impressive. It's certainly acceptable to let her know what you're doing on her behalf, but ratcheting up her anxiety level is not a good idea.

Here is a brief list of phrases that create anxiety, along with examples of what you can say instead.

WORDS THAT CREATE ANXIETY	WORDS THAT MAKE HER FEEL COMFORTABLE
I'm afraid that isn't going to work.	Let me see what I can do to make that work for you.
That's not our policy.	I'll talk to a few people, and see what we can work out. We want you to be happy.
You'll have to check with your mortgage broker.	I'd be happy to get that information for you.
There's usually a long wait.	I'll personally walk your application through our office.
We've never done that before.	Let's see if it's do-able.
You need to submit that by the 15th or it won't go through.	We can draw up the paperwork for you. Then you can approve it and we'll submit it.

There are other steps you can take to add to her peace of mind:

➤ A new customer usually gets a barrage of paper she may not understand. You can relieve her mind by identifying the most important documents as well as those that can be thrown away—and then organize them so that they're easy for her to find. Many banks and brokerages provide a three-ring binder for this purpose. Why not offer to help her assemble it?

➤ Keep items pending in her account somewhere that your assistant can easily access. Then if your customer calls concerning a missing document, for example, or the record for a funds transfer, your assistant can answer her questions if you are not available.

➤ Go to her, rather than asking her to come to you. Most men can't imagine how complicated it can be for a woman to carve out the time to visit her broker's office.

➤ Anticipate problems that could arise. For example, if she is likely to be out of town or otherwise unavailable at a crucial time, arrange for someone to have power of attorney.

If something goes wrong, make sure it's taken care of promptly. Apologize to her right away, even if it wasn't your fault. Taking personal responsibility will reinforce in her mind that you value your relationship with her and are doing whatever it takes to make it a happy one.

Pitfalls

➤ *Over-explaining.* Assume that she's a busy person, and limit explanations accordingly. Executing the sale may involve many steps, but unless she makes a specific request for information, she doesn't need to know all the details.

➤ *Losing your focus.* Stay involved. After-sale support is not something you can provide with half your brain engaged—not the kind of thoughtful and proactive help that will delight her and have her singing your praises to her friends and colleagues.

STAYING IN TOUCH

How to Build an Enhanced Relationship with Her and Hers

If you've been applying the concepts of this book to your women customers, by now you should be sitting on a veritable gold mine of potential new business.

As anyone in sales or marketing can tell you, the best customer is an old (i.e., existing) customer—for all the obvious reasons: you already have a relationship, she trusts you, you know what she needs, et c. There is also the cost angle: depending on the industry, it can cost anywhere from two to forty times more to acquire a new customer than to keep an old one.[1]

The next best customer is someone referred to you by an existing customer. Compared to customers developed through cold calling or direct marketing, referrals are always more cost-effective. They require less convincing, they make the decision to buy faster, they tend to generate repeat business, and they are themselves more likely to refer you to others.[2] And that's customers of both genders.

A satisfied woman customer is a veritable referral machine. In general, a woman will share her experiences more than a man will, and in more detail. She likes to help; if you have helped your woman customer, she will need

> *A satisfied woman customer is a veritable referral machine.*

[1] Rhonda Abrams, New Business from Old Clients, *Inc.com,* April 2002.
[2] Richard Banfield, *How Referral Marketing Can Grow Your Profits,* On Track Coaching & Consulting Inc., 2003.

little encouragement from you to let her friends and families know what you did for her, and how you can help them.

When she shares information about you with her friends, she's engaging in word-of-mouth marketing, the most important and compelling form of marketing communication. People perceive word-of-mouth messages to be credible, trustworthy, and without hidden motives. What's more, the recipients of word-of-mouth messages typically pass them on to other people they know.[3]

A satisfied woman customer is one of the most powerful and least appreciated generators of extraordinary sales results. Think of the complex lives women lead. Each of your women customers is a potential point of entry to several markets: family members, friends, colleagues, community organizations, and businesses.

In short, whatever you can do to sustain and enrich your relationship with her will be effort well spent, both in terms of the business she will give you and the connections she will create for you with people in her networks.

In addition to nurturing the relationship, one of the reasons we talk so much about going the extra mile for your women customers is that special treatment gives them something to talk about with other people. A woman we know went to a department store to buy her husband a blue shirt with a white collar. She'd seen one in their catalog and she knew he would like it, but the store was out of his size.

Seeing her disappointment, the saleswoman said, "If you can wait until tomorrow, I'll have something for you."

The next day wife went back to the store, and the saleswoman presented her with a blue shirt with a white collar in her husband's size. "That's fantastic!" said the wife. "Where'd you get it?"

[3] Michael Cafferky, *Let Your Customers Do the Talking*. Dearborn Trade, 1995.

"Actually, I made it," the saleswoman said. "I took home a blue shirt and a white shirt in the same style in his size. I replaced the blue collar on the blue shirt with the white collar from the white shirt. Voila! A blue shirt with a white collar."

That was years ago, and the woman is still dining out on this stellar example of a salesperson going the extra mile.

1. STAY IN TOUCH WITH HER—EVEN WHEN YOU DON'T WANT ANYTHING

Knowing how—and how often—to contact a woman customer is a delicate matter. On the one hand, women are busy. They can't afford to waste time in purposeless activity, and they will resent any implication on your part that they have unlimited available time. On the other hand, women like to know you're thinking about them, especially when you don't have anything to sell them.

There are two things about the D-gene that make contact a little easier. First, if you've been paying attention, you have discovered points of intersection between her life and interests and yours. Each one of these presents opportunities for maintaining and enhancing the relationship—sending her a book on a subject of common interest, for example, or letting her know about an upcoming event that you think she'd like.

> **BE REALISTIC ABOUT WHAT YOU CAN DO**
>
> *When you're just starting out, you'll probably have plenty of time to stay in touch. As you get more customers, you may have less time. This is when small-group events can work for you—as long as they feel personal.*

Second, women like to bond with each other. Women like to think of themselves as part of your family of customers. Here are some things you can do to foster this feeling:

> ➤ *A family holiday party.* One Midwestern broker has a party in his house each year during the holiday season. His customers can meet his wife and children, and each other.

"It's a very popular occasion," he said. "The women especially like to see where I live, and what my family is like. Some of my customers have seen my kids grow up. We've shared stories about school sports, raising teenagers, and now college."

➤ *Wine-tastings.* A broker we know in Florida holds wine-tastings with some of his women customers, and their snow-bird friends who visit during the winter. "I've been doing this for six years," he says. "It's never more than four or five people, eight at the most. I work with a wine shop to arrange different types of tastings—all Viogniers, maybe, or the wines from a specific region. We have nice hors d'oeuvres while an expert talks about what we're drinking. It's easy and very popular, and I get a lot of new business from it. I also catch up with my existing customers. They like it because it's a way for them to entertain their out-of-town guests."

➤ *Valentine celebration, with photos.* Two male brokers got together for Valentine's Day and invited their single women customers out for dessert and coffee. "We scheduled it for mid-afternoon, which meant the 12 women who came were mostly older and not working. They enjoyed meeting each other. We gave each woman a red rose, and at the end we took a photo of the group. We sent each woman a print, and Tom and I put framed prints in our offices. Last month I visited one of the women, and I noticed her photo was on her refrigerator."

➤ *A day at the spa.* We know of a woman broker who regularly invites her women customers to the local spa for a day of pampering. She gets a special deal from the spa by holding these events on their slowest day of the week.

Make it clear that you won't do any selling at gatherings like these; your only purpose is to stay in touch and build relationships.

Staying in touch doesn't have to be this elaborate. More modest suggestions include the following:

➤ Visit, phone, or send an email one week after a sale or transaction to make sure she's delighted with it—and to take care of any problems that may have come up.

➤ Send notes thanking her for her business.

➤ Return her calls within three hours, and always on the same day.

➤ Send a monthly newsletter with items of interest to women. Be sure to add a hand-written note or something else to personalize it.

➤ Send holiday and birthday cards. Personalize them in some way. Hint: don't send cards provided by your company—they're the opposite of personal.

➤ We heard of one broker who uses different types of envelopes to distinguish between personal correspondence and more routine mailings. "That way," he claims, "they're sure to open the letters I write directly to them."

2. KEEP HER ON YOUR CALENDAR

In your initial discussions with your customer, you may have determined the types of financial services she would need over time. To bring your business to the next level with her, it is a good idea to schedule periodic meetings in which you assess her satisfaction, catch up on any changes in her life, and how they have affected her financial needs.

Here again, your earlier efforts at female-focused listening can pay off. As children or grandchildren grow up, will they have tuition needs your customer may want to help with? Or, at the other end of the age spectrum, what about your customer's aging parents? Is she responsible for them? Does she need to make changes in her financial picture to make sure they are cared for? Your customer herself may be reaching the age at which she relies increasingly on her adult child or children. Wouldn't it help if you had a relationship with them?

At these meetings you can share any products or services she might need now, or in the future. At the same time, however, you should reaffirm your interest in being her long-term trusted business adviser. Any recommendations you make should support this role.

One idea to consider is sending her an anniversary card each year to commemorate the day she became your customer. Include a checklist of life changes that might prompt her to review her financial situation.

3. ENCOURAGE HER TO SUPPORT YOUR EFFORTS

Women love to support people who have provided excellent service to them. It's the nurturing part of the D-gene coming out. In other words, you don't need to push women to send you referrals; such hard-ball tactics could even backfire. On the other hand, because she's so busy, you might need to help her focus her efforts on your behalf. Emphasize your enthusiasm for your work, and your interest in helping others:

One of the things I enjoy about this job is being able to help people like you think through their financial future.

If you know other people I might be able to help, I hope you'll let me know.

4. TRAVEL IN THE CIRCLES SHE DOES

For obvious reasons, the most effective sales professionals are usually those who lead an active and varied life, have several interests they pursue, and come in contact with people from many different walks of life. All this helps them maintain a balanced outlook on their work. It also expands the pool of possible new customers, and raises the likelihood of crossing paths with existing customers.

Here are some ways you can express your interests in ways that will appeal to women:

> *Volunteer.* Women do a lot of volunteer work, and are impressed by men who do the same. What types of organizations or issues would you like to get involved in? Animal rights? Domestic abuse issues? Historical preservation? Nature conservation?

> *Learn about women's issues.* Read some books. Check out some newsletters. Listen to what the thought leaders have to say. You'll get a better sense of your present and potential women customers, and you may be able to do some good at the same time.

> *Work in your community.* Find local organizations that need your help, and join them. Make it your business to stay abreast of what's happening in your area: events, theatrical programs, exhibits, educational offerings, trips. You'll soon become known as the go-to guy for customers looking for a special class, a summer program for their tween-age child, or what to do with visiting relatives.

> *Stand for something.* If, in the course of your volunteer and community work, you discover a cause or an organization you feel strongly about, develop this interest. Follow your passion, as the saying goes. In time you will become identified with this interest, and people will be drawn to you because of it.

SELLING TO COUPLES

How to Connect with Husbands *and* Wives

Does decoding the D-gene help you sell to couples?

Absolutely. Understanding the D-gene will increase your awareness of what the woman might be thinking and feeling, and how you can best meet her needs and make her feel comfortable.

However, there is also the other spouse to consider. Together they present some special challenges. Some of these simply have to do with the fact you're having a conversation with a man and a woman at the same time. Others are created by the dynamics between a husband and wife—some predictable, others unique to each couple.

> **OUTSIDERS BEWARE!**
>
> *For many if not most couples, money is a vehicle for relating. A discussion of money, therefore, may not be only a discussion about money. It may be an arena for expressing the emotional dynamics of the relationship.*

Selling to a couple may be the biggest single selling challenge a sales professional faces. Small wonder: when you sell to a couple, you're dealing with two genders who:

> ➤ Communicate differently
>
> ➤ Relate to other people differently
>
> ➤ Take in and process information differently
>
> ➤ Make decisions differently

Appearances Are Usually Deceiving

When it comes to major purchases, more and more sales involve both spouses. Even though one spouse may appear to take the lead, you cannot assume he or she is the decision-maker. This is just one of the assumptions that can get you in trouble with a couple—as a D-gene-savvy salesman we'll call Ted found out.

Ted first talked to Penny, the wife, who was doing some preliminary research to find a financial adviser. "My husband has asked me to get some information from a few companies," she said over the phone, making it sound as if this whole exercise was primarily his idea. However, with what Ted had learned about the D-gene, he wasn't fooled.

Ted's first face-to-face meeting was with both spouses, Penny and Frank. At this meeting Penny didn't say much, leaving it to Frank to explain what they wanted, and to ask most of the questions. Knowing his way around a D-gene, Ted made a valiant effort to direct his remarks to both spouses, but the husband was so much more engaged—asking questions, offering opinions, apparently tracking right along with Ted—that despite Ted's best intentions he found himself focusing solely on Frank.

After several frustrating minutes of trying to speak to them both, Ted figured, "OK, I gave it my best shot. D-gene or no D-gene, this is obviously Frank's party, and Penny's just along for the ride." From that point on Ted zeroed in on the husband— bringing out the financial charts (which Ted pushed across the table in Frank's direction), the sports metaphors, and even permitting himself a little conspiratorial laugh when Frank made a joke at his wife's expense.

In subsequent calls to their home, Ted always asked to speak Frank, knowing how busy women are. However, when two weeks went by and they still hadn't made a decision, Ted found himself on the phone with Penny, who told him they'd decided to go with another financial adviser—someone whose office was closer to her husband's. Ted recognized this statement for what it was: an attempt on Penny's part to extricate herself without hurting Ted's feelings, and he didn't try to convince her to reconsider. He realized any sale was dead in the water.

What Went Wrong?

Let's take a look at how Ted blew the sale. First of all, the fact that the wife didn't say much should have told Ted almost nothing. Many women will defer to their husbands in public. They may have strong opinions, they may have more technical knowledge, they may be movers and shakers in their professional lives—but in public they may feel more comfortable letting their husbands take the lead. Do they not want to appear "unfeminine"? Do they fear damaging their husbands' fragile male egos? Who knows? For our purposes, it doesn't really matter. The point is, her reticence seldom has much to do with her role in the buying process. Ted knew this, and if he were talking only to Penny, he might have been able to use his female-focused listening skills to draw her out and establish a relationship. Frank's presence, however, threw him off.

What about Frank? Why was he so much more engaged in the conversation than his wife was? Was he more interested? More comfortable talking about financial matters? Was this something he wanted more than she did? Was he the decision-maker? Maybe. Maybe he was trying to show Ted (and his wife) that he was just as much of a financial expert as Ted. Of course, once Ted gave up trying to include her in the conversation, he and Frank did start to connect—"How about those Yankees?"—so much, in fact, that Penny began to feel left out.

And what about Ted's laughing at the joke Frank made at his wife's expense? And always asking for Frank when he called their house? How big a negative impact did these behaviors have?

It's hard to say, although our best guess is that Ted lost the sale at that first meeting. "I liked that guy," the husband might have said to his wife on their way home. "What did you think?"

"I don't know," she probably said. "He seemed OK on the phone, but there was something about him in the meeting I didn't warm up to."

If you think that Frank will dare work with Ted after Penny drops a remark like that, you need to go back to Relationships 101. Think about it: if Ted made a mistake—or Penny thought he did—Frank would never hear the end of it. And if one of their investments went south, who do you think Penny would blame? She might not be the kind of person to say "I told you so," but both spouses would know the phrase was hovering out there.

Guiding a Couple's Buying Experience

Your goal for managing a conversation with a husband and wife should be to find a way to communicate with both of them, identify and build on areas of agreement, and avoid getting caught up in the dynamics between them. It's a good idea early in your conversation with the couple to ask each person to state the reason they came to see you. This will give you a good idea of how in sync they are; if they can't agree on a broad generality, chances are the discussion isn't going to get easier once you get into specifics.

If they're in agreement now but disagree as the process continues, you can refer back to this common goal to help get the discussion back on track. For example, if the spouses have reached a sticking point over where to invest their money, you can remind them that they came in with the goal of having enough money in eight years to pay for their daughter's college tuition in eight years' time, or whatever their objective was.

Ask each spouse for his or her objective in coming to see you. You don't want to underscore differences, but it will help you to know how they differ in their approaches to investing, their relative comfort levels with risk, as well as any preferences for certain types of investments.

As your discussions continue, take every opportunity to restate their positions in terms that highlight areas of agreement: "It's important to both of you to find something with a higher rate of return than you're now getting," or "although you have different ideas about which industries to invest in, you both feel more comfortable with mutual funds than individual company stocks."

If they agree with each other but not with you, feel free to represent your point of view. If they disagree with each other, stand back. Don't try to convince them of either position. Instead, think of yourself as an educator or a facilitator—bringing up relevant information, summarizing their positions as they evolve, and, again, always looking for areas of agreement.

Some Other Do's and Don'ts

Dealing with some couples can feel as if you're walking through a minefield, but the fact is, especially in the field of financial services, many of your customers are couples (even if you only deal with the male half) and you will need to know how to navigate successfully. Fortunately, there are some guidelines you can follow that will help you increase your chances of success—even with the toughest of couples.

> ➤ *Shake hands with both of them.* Don't lose any sleep over the "shaking hands" issue. It doesn't matter whose hand you shake first. Start with the person who is closest to you. Don't make a fool of yourself by going around the husband to shake the wife's hand first—or vice versa.

> ➤ *Until they tell you differently, assume both spouses are equally involved in all phases of the buying process.* They may not appear to be, and in fact when it comes to finances, one spouse usually ends up doing more of the work. The question is, where does the decision-making power lie? Who

has the power to kill the deal? Until you know for sure, it's easier, and safer, to assume they are equal partners.

➤ *Pay equal attention to each spouse.* This isn't always easy, especially if one spouse is much more responsive than the other, but if you can't figure out a way to do it, you'll quickly get yourself in hot water. If you pay more attention to the wife, for example, she'll be sensitive to the poor treatment her husband is getting, and will side with him against you.

If you pay more attention to the man, on the other hand, she'll assume you're ignoring her because she is a woman. As we saw with Ted, ignoring the woman tends to be a deal-breaker, although neither spouse may ever say so.

➤ *Think about visuals.* Use what you know about the D-gene to make sure your visuals appeal to women as well as men. Also, if you use charts or brochures, make sure both spouses can easily see them. Many salespeople have two sets prepared, one for each spouse. If you decide to do this, by all means prepare them ahead of time. If you stop the meeting to get a second set of materials, one of the spouses will think he or she was an after-thought. For your sake, we hope it's not the wife.

➤ *Use inclusive language when you answer their questions.* Even though one spouse may have asked a question, frame your answer in a way that will appeal to the other spouse as well. Use phrases like "both of you," or "your family." Make eye contact with both spouses as you speak. Whenever possible, create bridges back to what both spouses said. Keep the focus on both of them.

➤ *Beware of slipping into your male default mode.* Even though you may have mastered female-friendly listening, focusing on the relationship, and all the other D-gene skills, they can seem a little awkward when you're talking to a

man as well as a woman. Some salesmen feel the need to
let the man know they are still "one of the guys," and also
that they are not hitting on the man's wife. You can
safely forget about these concerns; they are almost certainly all in your head. The bigger danger is connecting
with the husband in a way that excludes the wife.

➤ *Never provide the husband with information or a "goodie" you
don't also offer the wife.* Some car dealership service departments automatically offer a man a loaner car, whereas
they will give a woman one only if she asks for it. If this
happens to a husband and wife, they'll both be angry—
she for the obvious reasons, he on her behalf, and because
he knows every time this dealership comes up in conversation, he's going to have to listen to her complain about
how unfair it is.

➤ *Never turn her down when she requests something, and then
reverse yourself when her husband calls.* You don't want to
leave the impression that you take him more seriously
than you take her. If you won't go to the trouble to get a
certain set of figures for her but you will for him, that's
exactly the impression you will leave

➤ *Don't try to psych out their relationship.* You can't. No one
knows what goes on behind closed doors, but you can be
sure it's more than meets the eye. Your safest position is
simply to treat them both as your customers.

➤ *Never—ever—take sides.* Did you ever have a friend who
told you he and his wife had separated? And you offered
your support by saying, in effect, that you never liked her
very much, only—oops!—to have them get back
together? In a way, this is what happened to Ted when he
joined Frank in laughing at his wife.

Taking sides—or appearing to take sides, which has the
same effect—is easier to fall into than you might think.

You're taking sides when:

- You support the husband as he tries to convince his wife to accept your recommendation.

- You correct one spouse.

- You nod, smile, or in some other nonverbal way, let the couple know which spouse you agree with.

- You agree with a spouse's opinion of a certain restaurant, and then discover that the other spouse has the opposite opinion.

➤ *Leave them alone.* When a couple disagrees, it's a good idea for you to retire from the scene and give them time to talk in private. In this way you can avoid getting sucked into the middle of an argument. Besides, it may be easier for them to reach agreement without the presence of a third party.

GETTING *RICH*

This book is about how to get RICH selling banking and brokerage services to women, right? That's what the title implies. So is that all there is to it? Now that you've read the book, you'll be living the lavish lifestyle—buying a bigger home, driving a luxury car and vacationing with the rich and famous?

It Takes Practice

Actually, there's one more thing that's required. It's important and something you'll need to take seriously. So just to lighten up a little, have you heard the one about the visitor who approached a native New Yorker on 5th Avenue and asked him, "Tell me, how do you get to Carnegie Hall?" Without breaking stride, the New Yorker responded, "practice, practice, practice." Okay, it's an old joke, but it makes the point. How many world-class musicians, artists, and athletes have been able to improve their performance simply by reading books on the subject?

Right. Zero. In other words, now that you've read about how to sell to women, it's time to go out and start putting what you know to work—testing the skills and concepts in this book, noticing how your customers respond, and making whatever adjustments seem necessary to get the results you're looking for. You won't change completely overnight—and you may feel awkward at first—but as these new behaviors become more comfortable, you will begin to notice positive results.

The key is to find the practice mode that works best for you. For some people, putting the concepts of this book into practice will require nothing more than a series of small adjustments. For others, it will require a fundamental shift in how they think and how they sell.

That's why in this book we have presented the principles and big-picture skills as well as individual examples of D-gene-friendly actions. Some readers will learn by internalizing the principles, which will lead them to individual behaviors more or less automatically. Others, by trying out individual behaviors, will eventually come to an adoption of the underlying principles.

On the Job

If you're serious about increasing your sales by expanding your base of women customers, there are several ways you can set up on-the-job learning experiences for yourself.

> ➤ *Go back through the book and identify a chapter that focuses on an area you would like to improve.* List two or three of the bulleted points in the chapter that strike you as especially important. Next to each point, identify a place where you could use that skill. Try it in a real situation. Evaluate how successful you were and decide what you need to do differently the next time.

> ➤ *Find a colleague who has read the book.* Choose a skill you'd each like to improve, and make a commitment to practice. After a few trial sales situations, get together and discuss what happened. Trade advice on what to do differently the next time.

> ➤ *Set yourself a private goal of increasing your sales to women by a specific amount in a six-month time period.* During this

time keep track of how well you perform the skills in each of the five competencies, and where your greatest challenges are. If you meet your goal, take a few minutes to decide which skills made the difference for you. Then set a more challenging goal for the next six months.

Me? Practice?

PLACE: *United Center Arena in Chicago.*

TIME: *6:20 P.M.*

At 8:05 the Chicago Bulls will be playing, but now there are fewer than a hundred fans in their seats.

On the court stands a six-foot-six-inch player wearing number 23. He is standing with his back to the basket, about thirteen feet out. Next to him is a rack of basketballs. He reaches for a ball, dribbles, launches himself into the air away from the basket, turns, and shoots while still in the air. He grabs another ball and does it again. And again. Jump, turn, shoot. Jump, turn, shoot.

The player is Michael Jordan, during his last week as an active player, and he is practicing his turnaround jumper. It is his signature shot. The other players? They're nowhere to be seen. They're taping their ankles, drinking soft drinks, talking to their agents or reviewing their contracts.

Out there on the court, Number 23 continues to practice. It's been forty minutes now, and the stands are beginning to fill up, but his focus is absorbed by what he's doing. Jump, turn, shoot. Jump, turn, shoot.

If the world's best basketball player at the top of his power sees the need to practice his signature shot for forty minutes before a game, then who can say that hard work and practice are not necessary at every point in our careers, no matter how successful we are?

In this book we have provided you the skills and principles you will need to achieve success selling financial services to women. Making it happen is up to you. Like Michael Jordan, you have to want success enough to be willing to work hard. You have to keep practicing and learning. It worked for Michael Jordan. It can work for you.

FIRST THE MONEY, NOW THE GIRL

For Men Only

So far, in selling banking and brokerage services to women, we've concentrated on helping you get more money. Now it's time to help you get (or keep) the girl.

Can the skills in this book also help you improve your personal relationships with the opposite sex?

You can bet on it.

If you're like the men in our workshops, you've probably already been mentally trying some of these concepts with your wife or girlfriend. So that's how she really thinks! No wonder she drives me crazy! No wonder *I* drive *her* crazy!

We'll never forget the participant in one of our seminars who came back late after the lunch break. "Sorry," he said, "I've been on the phone with my wife, apologizing for the last 15 years."

Understanding the D-gene does not mean you have to accept the blame for everything that happens in a relationship. Nor will it smooth out every rough patch you and your significant other experience. However, it sure can clear away a lot of futile arguments.

For Stan, a California broker, his first post-D-gene interaction had to do with a story his wife had wanted to tell him the night before. Here's the dialog as he remembers it:

SHE: *Did you hear what happened to the Harners?*

HE: *No, what?*

SHE: *Well, I saw Marylou at the store today, and she seemed a little different. Some people can't hide their feelings, you know what I mean¿*

HE: *Not exactly, but—*

SHE: *(interrupting) Well, with Marylou you can always tell how she's feeling just by looking at her.*

HE: *Uh huh. So what happened¿*

SHE: *Well, you knew they'd been in couples therapy.*

HE: *No . . .*

SHE: *Yes, I told you last week!*

HE: *You did¿ OK, so . . . what happened¿*

SHE: *Marylou said Doug has been expressing a lot of angry feelings in therapy, and she got frightened. Apparently Doug has a really dark side. I never thought of him in those terms, did you¿*

HE: *You mean he hit her¿*

SHE: *No . . .*

HE: *What happened, then¿!*

SHE: *I'm trying to tell you!!*

HE: *Are they getting a divorce¿ Is that it¿*

SHE: *No!*

HE: *(checking his watch) OK, look. I've got a lot of calls to return. Can we just cut to the chase here¿*

"As soon as I heard myself say 'cut to the chase,' I realized we had a classic D-gene situation on our hands," he said. "I'm *always* telling her to cut to the chase, and she *always* wants to give me the details. Now I realize it's just the damned D-gene."

Understanding alone won't automatically solve issues like this, but it makes them easier to deal with because it removes the element of blame: Stan's wife is not disorganized, nor is Stan cold-hearted. It's the D-gene. With any luck, once you understand the D-gene, you can both stop wasting so much energy trying to change each other.

A Whole New Light

There are many couples who would have very little to say if they stopped trying to change each other. Spousal Change, in fact, may be one of our most popular marital pastimes—especially early in a marriage—and it's one which women seem to approach with more fervor and a greater sense of purpose than men.

Think of a common "issue" between you and your wife or girl-friend. To what extent is it influenced by the D-gene? If you stopped trying to change her, what could *you* do about it?

Here's a list to get you started:

THE "ISSUE"	THE INFLUENCE OF THE D-GENE	WHAT YOU CAN DO
HE: *What's your point?!* SHE: *I'm trying to tell you. Stop rushing me!*	Context is important to a woman, while outcome is important to a man.	Sit back and relax. Don't look at your watch.
SHE: *You always interrupt me!* HE: *I do not!*	Although women's speech patterns allow interruptions, they don't like to be interrupted. To a man, interruptions are normal parts of any lively conversation.	Zip your lip. (This gets easier with practice.)
HE: *If he's not punished, he'll never learn.* SHE: *Everything is black or white to you!*	Women tend to consider personal circumstances when making judgments. Men tend to think in abstract, right-wrong terms.	Ask yourself how you would like to be judged, and be grateful that some members of the human race may be willing to show you some mercy.

THE "ISSUE"	THE INFLUENCE OF THE D-GENE	WHAT YOU CAN DO
SHE: *You're not listening!* **HE:** *I am, too!*	Women look for signs of active listening— nodding, smiling, commenting, while men tend to listen passively.	Respond. Nod. Say "uh huh."
SHE: *We need to talk.* **HE:** *Can we do it later? I'm trying to watch the game.*	Women derive more of their identity from relationships than men do.	Hit the "pause" button and give her your full attention. You can watch the game later. (This assumes you own that indispensable marital aid known as TiVo.)

Share the Knowledge

One important difference to keep in mind is that your wife or girlfriend is not your customer. She is a full partner in your relationship. If you want to collaborate in a serious way with a special woman in your life, she will need to understand the D-gene, too. Give her the book, and ask her to read Chapter 3, "Decoding the D-Gene," and Chapter 4, "Not Until She Trusts You."

We've found that when you have conflict, a little humor often helps. Here are some humorous men-made rules for women that we found circulating on the Internet.

> ➤ Sunday sports on TV are a force of nature, like the tides, or the phases of the moon. Don't get in the way.

> ➤ Ask directly for what you want. Hints do not work, even "obvious" hints. Just say it.

> ➤ So, for example, if we ask what is wrong and you say "nothing," we will act like nothing's wrong. We know

you think something's wrong, but we resent the energy required to tease it out of you.

➤ If you come to us with a problem, don't be surprised if we try to solve it for you. If it's only sympathy you want, make sure you tell us that. Otherwise, you might want to talk to your girlfriends.

➤ Christopher Columbus did not need directions and neither do we.

➤ I *am* in shape. Round is a shape.

After you've had a good laugh, have a good conversation. See what ideas *she* may have to deal with the D-gene. She may be eager to change a few of her own behaviors since she highly values your relationship.

Get Creative

"The only time I have ever had a man pay attention to me—I mean, really pay attention, was when he was trying to get me into bed," Marsha said. "Not just the candy and flowers stuff, but listening and being attentive and remembering what I say. Of course, then you sleep with him and everything changes."

Marsha is not the first woman to make this observation. What's interesting here, however, is the parallel she suggests to the selling process. Once a prospect is wooed and won, do you take her for granted? Or, as a bank customer we quoted in Chapter 2 put it, "Is it only their new customers who get special treatment and better rates?"

If you take a look at the five principles of trust-based selling, you will see how directly they apply to a personal relationship:

➤ Think relationship, not product.

➤ Respect her, her time, and her timing.

➤ Understand her on her own terms.

> ➤ Surpass her every expectation.

> ➤ Telegraph confidence.

Think about it: To sell effectively to a woman you need to do and say things to demonstrate that:

> ➤ You value your relationship with her above any sale.

> ➤ You have confidence and competence, yet you never manipulate or hurry her into a decision.

> ➤ You consider her a special individual with unique needs that cannot be satisfied with cookie-cutter solutions. She can expect special treatment from you.

> ➤ Because you listen carefully and remember what she tells you, you understand her situation, and offer help that is best for her in both the short and long term.

> ➤ You know how to adapt yourself to her timing, along with her preferred style of communicating and decision-making.

> ➤ Whenever you can, you will create solutions that will surprise and delight her, and give her stories about your creativity and thoughtfulness that she can regale her friends with.

If you show this list to your wife or girlfriend, we guarantee she'll say, "Hey, I'd like some of that!"

Trying out these ideas with your wife or girlfriend is a safe way to try out new approaches, fine-tune your new skills, and get the kind of honest feedback you could never get from a customer. In any event, once you begin to put the material in this book into practice at work, you will notice improvement in all your relationships with women—whether you make a conscious choice to apply them in your private life or not.

In the final analysis, everybody wins. You increase your sales. Your women customers form a relationship with a salesperson they trust to do right by them. And you can enjoy relationships with the important women in your life—wife, girlfriend, mother, daughter—free of those frictions and conflicts the D-gene can produce.

ABOUT MADDOX SMYE'S
HOW TO GET **RICH** SELLING TO WOMEN
SKILLS DEVELOPMENT PROGRAM

Maddox Smye, LLC, was founded in 1993 with the mandate to help companies convert more women shoppers into buyers, long-term customers and vocal advocates. The stated mission is to "help leading edge companies close more sales by building enduring relationships with women."

Firm founder, Rebecca Maddox spent over 15 years researching and developing an understanding of what women value and how women think, shop, decide, and buy. Collaborating together, Rebecca and co-founder, Marti Smye, Ph.D., renowned organizational behaviorist, used the research to pioneer a scientific approach to selling to women that consistently translates into incremental, measurable sales for a blue-chip roster of client companies.

Maddox Smye's 12-week Skills Development Program is based on a one-of-a-kind, proprietary sales audit system that culminates in an individualized, confidential report on 63 criteria necessary to proficiently sell and serve women customers. With "real" data as the baseline, sales professionals attend a one-day workshop introducing the five core competencies required to become a woman's trusted advisor. The program continues with 11 additional weeks of coaching and clinics, using a wide range of technology and tools that aid participants in adapting behavioral skills and producing measurable results.

For more information on the *Maddox Smye How to Get RICH Selling to Women Skills Development System,* please visit our website, www.maddoxsmye.com.

ABOUT MADDOX SMYE'S
KEYNOTES AND PRESENTATIONS

A presentation or keynote address by Rebecca Maddox, MBA, CPA, and founding principal of Maddox Smye is an effective way for your organization to gain valuable insights and information from the last 15 years of research and development that gave birth to the Maddox Smye *How To Get RICH Selling to Women* philosophy and methodology.

Rebecca Maddox has emerged as the definitive voice on gender-focused selling to women. She is a recognized member of the National Speakers Association and one of the most dynamic and entertaining keynote speakers you will hear. Rebecca speaks weekly, around the world, to audiences representing thirty-six different industries. A sampling of her keynote topics include:

How to Get RICH Selling to Women

In this interactive and energizing presentation, you will learn the five commonsense principles that hold the key to building T.R.U.S.T. with women and the five core competencies required to close sales with women, the application of which has been reported to increase personal revenue by 45%.

To Women, You Are Not a Billion Dollar Corporation, You Are a Guy Named Dave!

Selling to women is a science, requiring both knowledge and action. Rebecca provides the knowledge—by introducing the 5-key competencies and the accompanying behaviors required to close sales to women. Your sales team provides the action—by implementing the strategies and tools from this presentation to experience immediate and significant results.

The New Frontier: From Competitive Advantage to Competitive Necessity

With women having responsibility for 89% of purchases today, if you still consider them a niche market you're already behind. Every year more sales are going to come from a purse and not a pocket in every consumer market. In this compelling presentation, Rebecca will help you position your sales force to get in the lead, close more sales to women and build the enduring relationships that result in loyalty and referrals.

For more information on Maddox Smye keynotes and presentations, please visit our website, www.maddoxsmye.com.

SHARE THE MESSAGE OF

HOW TO GET RICH SELLING BANKING AND BROKERAGE SERVICES TO WOMEN!

WITH YOUR CLIENTS AND YOUR SALES TEAMS

To get information or order additional copies visit our website at: www.maddoxsmye.com

OR WRITE US AT:
300 5th Avenue South
Suite 101, Box 420
Naples, Florida 34102